DAVID WENTZ

When Church Stops Working

Meeting With God in Your Living Room

First published by Doing Christianity 2022

Copyright © 2022 by David Wentz

All rights reserved. No part of this publication may be reproduced, stored or transmitted in any form or by any means, electronic, mechanical, photocopying, recording, scanning, or otherwise without written permission from the publisher. It is illegal to copy this book, post it to a website, or distribute it by any other means without permission.

David Wentz asserts the moral right to be identified as the author of this work.

David Wentz has no responsibility for the persistence or accuracy of URLs for external or third-party Internet Websites referred to in this publication and does not guarantee that any content on such Websites is, or will remain, accurate or appropriate.

Unless otherwise marked, Scriptures are taken from the HOLY BIBLE, NEW LIVING TRANSLATION (NLT): Scriptures taken from the HOLY BIBLE, NEW LIVING TRANSLATION, Copyright© 1996, 2004, 2007 by Tyndale House Foundation. Used by permission of Tyndale House Publishers, Inc., Carol Stream, Illinois 60188. All rights reserved. Used by permission.

Scriptures marked NASB are taken from the NEW AMERICAN STANDARD (NAS): Scripture taken from the NEW AMERICAN STANDARD BIBLE®, copyright© 1960, 1962, 1963, 1968, 1971, 1972, 1973, 1975, 1977, 1995 by The Lockman Foundation. Used by permission.

Scriptures marked NIV are taken from the NEW INTERNATIONAL VERSION (NIV): Scripture taken from THE HOLY BIBLE, NEW INTERNATIONAL VERSION ®. Copyright© 1973, 1978, 1984, 2011 by Biblica, Inc.TM. Used by permission of Zondervan

First edition

ISBN: 978-1-7331285-6-8

This book was professionally typeset on Reedsy. Find out more at reedsy.com

Dedicated to all the faithful Christians who continue to believe in Jesus and seek his presence, in or out of a conventional church.

Where two or three gather together as my followers, I am there among them.

—Jesus (Matthew 18:20)

Contents

Introduction	ii
I How Did We Get to This Place?	
1 The Presence of God	3
2 Conventional, Institutionalized, Ecclesia	7
3 The First Jesus Followers	13
4 How Christianity Spread	19
5 How Did Biblical Ecclesia Become Institutionalized Church?	27
II So What Do We Do Now?	
6 Why Should Christians Gather Together?	35
7 Here's What It Might Look Like	55
8 Don't We Need a Preacher?	74
9 How to Start	87
10 What If It Really Takes Off?	101
Epilogue: You Can Do This!	115
Appendix 1: Sermons in a Nutshell	117
Appendix 2: Potential Problems	129
About the Author	144
Also by David Wentz	146

Introduction

If right now you find yourself struggling with organized religion, know this: so did Jesus. – *Facebook meme posted by The Weird Preacher, from an unknown source*

There has to be more to God's idea of church than the bureaucratic institutions most of us know, and there has to be more to God than we find in most churches.

Jesus promised, *Where two or three gather together as my followers, I am there among them* (Matthew 18:20). God is always with us, but sometimes there is a special presence. It's usually not overwhelming glory and power, but it is something you can sense. My best description is a combination of peace and expectation that is almost heavy in the air. Our culture in general hasn't experienced it enough to develop the proper words, but you can learn to recognize it.

Why don't we experience that sense of God's presence more often, especially in church? Part of it is because we have never been taught what it is. But often the reason may be that we are not fulfilling the conditions of the promise. Too often, following Jesus gets lost in all the other things going on, both good and bad.

Singing a few songs, learning a bit of theology, occasionally doing some kind of community work to feel good about — is that kind of church experience all God wants us to know of him? I don't think so.

Sex scandals and coverups, church splits and court battles, judgmentalism and gossip and cliques and partisan political posturing and endless appeals for money – is that what God had in mind when he invented church? I don't think so.

And I'm not alone. Perhaps the fastest growing group of Christians in America is those who used to go to church, but don't anymore. They still believe in God, they still pray and read the Bible, they still consider themselves Christians. They just don't go to church. For them, church has stopped working.

If that's you, don't worry, I'm not trying to get you back in the pews. I identify with what you're feeling – and I was a pastor for 38 years. I'm here now to assure you that you can be a healthy, connected, functioning part of the Body of Christ – part of the church in the Biblical sense – without being part of the bureaucratic institution that too many American churches have become.

What do I mean when I say "stopped working?" I mean that, for whatever reason, church is not doing whatever you need it to do for you. It doesn't make you feel better. It doesn't help you cope. It doesn't help you grow. It doesn't help you sense God's love. It might still do these things for the rest of the congregation, but it no longer does for you.

Not that church should be all about making people feel good. It's not supposed to be a party or a social club. In fact, many people have given up on church precisely because the focus was too much on pleasing people, and not enough on connecting with God. But if you really are connecting with God, and the people you spend time with are connecting with God, then it just naturally will have a positive impact on your life. The God part and the you part and the people part should all go together. When they don't, church has stopped working. And people who stop attending are not rejecting God's plan for his people, but a human institutionalized distortion of it.

This book is not about fixing the institutionalized church. There are plenty of books about that. This book is for ordinary Christian believers who have given up on church, but don't want to give up on God or their Christian friends.

The Lord's Prayer teaches us to call God, "Our Father" (Matthew 6:9). The Bible promises, *To all who believed him and accepted him, he gave the right to become children of God* (John 1:12). Christians are not just God's people; we're

God's family. Every time we come together it's a family reunion.

Somebody says, "You've got that right. I was raised in the most dysfunctional family you ever saw, and that's just what my old church was like."

I hear you. Believe me, I've been there. But something is only dysfunctional because it's not functioning the way it's supposed to. The Bible says God is good, God is faithful and God always gives justice. Most of all, it says God is love (John 4:8). God's family, done right, reflects those characteristics.

Where two or three gather together as my followers, I am there among them (Matthew 18:20). That is a promise from Jesus. This book will show you how you and a few friends can put that promise into action.

Throughout history and around the world, probably more Christians have gathered with God in homes and other private places than in church buildings. Even today, in places like China and Iran, millions meet privately in home fellowships. In America, one of the fastest growing expressions of Christianity is the house church movement. You can meet in person, online, or both simultaneously. However you choose, it will transform your life. I know. It happened to me.

When my wife Paula and I graduated from college, I was recruited as an engineer by Ford Motor Company. We moved from the University of Virginia to suburban Detroit. The closest people we knew lived 500 miles away. The Lord led us to a small Church of the Nazarene congregation. There we and a few other young Christians decided to start getting together every week to talk about the Bible. The pastor wasn't involved. None of us had any theological education. We didn't follow any kind of program. We just did part of what I describe in this book. It only lasted about a year and a half before we moved to California. Yet as we look back, Paula and I agree: even though I was a pastor for 38 years and have degrees from three different seminaries, the warmest Christian friendships and the greatest spiritual growth either of us has ever experienced happened when we and those other ordinary Christians got together in each other's homes.

As I said, we only did part of what I describe in this book. Our church activities took care of the rest. Yet our home Bible study gave us the close personal relationships that just can't happen in a Sunday service, and the spiritual growth that can't be had from even the best sermons.

Bible studies and prayer groups are good and important, but they can only fulfill a few of the seven purposes for which God calls his people together (see Chapter 6). All seven are needed to accomplish God's purposes in us and the world. This book will show you how you and a few friends, meeting in someone's home, can fulfill them all — often better than most conventional churches can.

Please understand. I'm not saying conventional churches are bad. Most of them do wonderful work in people's lives and communities. Millions of people attend faithfully and find it a blessing. Good for them! I pray God's blessings on all of them.

But you are not one of those people anymore, or you wouldn't be reading this book. Fortunately, when the Bible says, *Let us not neglect our meeting together* (Hebrews 10:25), it doesn't necessarily mean sitting in a special building listening to an ordained preacher. That is certainly not the only way to be God's church, and it may not even be the best way. These next pages will show you what just might be the best way. It's not hard!

Part One lays a little groundwork by looking at how the modern institution called church is different from Christian gatherings in New Testament times, and how it got that way. Part Two gives step by step guidance about how you and a few friends can gather as followers of Jesus and experience his presence among you, without all the institutional trappings.

Each chapter ends with discussion questions. Here's my idea: ask a few friends to read this book with you, like a book club. Talk about it, using the questions as a starting point. By the time you are done, if you like what you've read, you'll have a ready-made group to try it out. If you don't, at least you will have had some interesting conversations.

Before we go on, I have two requests. The first one might be kind of personal. You used to go to church. You must have found something there that kept you coming back: peace, healing, friends, good teaching, a connection with God, a chance to use your talents, a chance to give back. Somebody or something took all that away from you. It's only natural to feel angry or bitter about that. But you're reading this book because you know there's something more than "only natural." There's the supernatural power of God.

Somebody said holding a grudge is like drinking poison and hoping it makes the other person sick. So here's the first request: ask God, by his supernatural grace, to help you love the person or group or institution that hurt you. You don't have to feel like loving them; God doesn't command us to have certain feelings. And you don't have to tell them, unless they ask. Just make a decision to love them, stop dwelling on it, and move on to the good things God has planned for you. I promise you'll feel better.

My second request is not so much for you, but it might help someone else. If you haven't already, please let the pastor know why you stopped coming to church. I can tell you from experience, good pastors notice when someone stops coming, and they care, and they can get discouraged. A card or email will do if you don't want to talk in person. If it was something the pastor said or did, let them know – they may not even be aware of it. And if it wasn't their fault, they are probably feeling the conflict even more than you do. An encouraging word, even from someone who has left, might make their day.

Now let's get started.

I

How Did We Get to This Place?

1

The Presence of God

Where two or three gather together as my followers, I am there among them.
— Matthew 18:20

A basic attribute of God, according to theologians, is omnipresence. That means God is always everywhere. One of the most beautiful and reassuring promises of the Bible describes it this way.

> *I can never escape from your Spirit! I can never get away from your presence! If I go up to heaven, you are there; if I go down to the grave, you are there. If I ride the wings of the morning, if I dwell by the farthest oceans, even there your hand will guide me, and your strength will support me.* (Psalm 139:7–10)

We know that God is everywhere, all the time. Ephesians 1:23 says, *Jesus fills all things everywhere with himself.* Yet somehow God wants to be with us, his children, in a special way.

God's desire has always been to live among his people. When Israel wandered in the wilderness, God told Moses, *Have the people of Israel build me a holy sanctuary so I can live among them* (Exodus 25:8).

When the Hebrews conquered the Promised Land and started living in houses, God approved David's plan to build a house where God could live. It was called the Temple, and God filled it with his presence (2 Chronicles 6:1). For the next thousand years, a series of temples in Jerusalem were the focus of God living among his people.

Unfortunately, somewhere between Solomon and Jesus, many Hebrews lost their understanding of what it meant to be God's chosen people. They forgot God chose them as messengers to invite the whole world into his family. Instead, they began to believe God chose them to be the only members of his family. Instead of welcoming other nations, they scorned them.

So God started again, with Jesus. But this time membership in the family wasn't by genes, but by choice. The Bible says, *Abraham's physical descendants are not necessarily children of God. Only the children of the promise are considered to be Abraham's children* (Romans 9:8). The "children of the promise" are all who put their faith in Jesus. *To all who believed him and accepted him, he gave the right to become children of God* (John 1:12).

God so longs to live among his people that when we die, God takes us to live with him until the end of time. And at the end of time, when everything is put the way God wants it, where will God live? With his people. *I heard a loud shout from the throne, saying, "Look, God's home is now among his people! He will live with them, and they will be his people. God himself will be with them"* (Revelation 21:3).

Membership in the family of God is open to everyone, regardless of their ancestry, who puts their faith in Jesus. And our loving Father has commanded us to bring as many people into the family as will accept the invitation. When we do that, we become the fulfillment of God's desire to live among his people. *Don't you realize that all of you together are the temple of God and that the Spirit of God lives in you?* (1 Corinthians 3:16).

God is not looking for a place to live. He has that in heaven. God is longing for a group of people to live with. God's plan in creating human beings was that we would be his family. Fulfilling that plan is why God wants Christians to gather together — because he wants to gather with us.

Sometimes the presence of God is more than a theological concept. Sometimes it's almost tangible. I bet you've said it yourself: "I could feel the touch of God." Or, "God really visited us today." That is called the manifest presence of God, when God chooses to manifest himself in a special way we can recognize.

That is what Jesus was talking about when he promised to be among his gathered followers. But it's a sad fact that many Christians have a hard time sensing God's presence in their church services.

Often that is because they haven't learned or been trained in how to recognize it. The Bible says, *solid food is for the mature, who because of practice have their senses trained to discern good and evil* (Hebrews 5:14, NASB). People may be aware of a certain kind of feeling or atmosphere in a room, but if they have never been taught, they might not recognize it as the presence of God.

Or they may never have been taught to quiet their souls enough to be aware of God's presence. *Be still, and know that I am God!* (Psalm 46:10).

But all too often, when people don't sense God's presence in church, the problem lies with the church.

When we sense the presence of Jesus, what we are sensing is his spirit, also known as the Holy Spirit. It has been said that the Holy Spirit is a gentleman. He will never force himself upon anyone. Instead, one of the biblical images for the Holy Spirit is a dove. Doves are gentle and quiet, and ready to take flight at any moment.

On the day of Pentecost, the Holy Spirit manifested himself somewhat differently.

> *Suddenly, there was a sound from heaven like the roaring of a mighty windstorm, and it filled the house where they were sitting. Then, what looked like flames or tongues of fire appeared and settled on each of them.* (Acts 2:2–3)

However, that kind of thing is very rare. Much more often, he is a *still, small voice* (1 Kings 19:12).

The apostle Paul wrote to the Christians meeting in home groups in Thessalonica, a city in modern-day Greece, *Do not stifle the Holy Spirit* (1 Thessalonians 5:19). Some church services are so pre-planned and tightly timed that the Spirit of Jesus could not get a word in edgewise if he wasn't already on the program. In many church services there is hardly a moment not already filled.

F. W. Faber wrote,

> There is hardly ever a complete silence in our soul. God is whispering to us well nigh incessantly. Whenever the sounds of the world die out in the soul, or sink low, then we hear these whisperings of God. He is always whispering to us, only we do not always hear, because of the noise, hurry, and distraction which life causes as it rushes on.

Unfortunately, that noise, hurry, and distraction can happen in a church service as easily as anywhere else.

Sometimes we stifle the Holy Spirit and won't let him talk. Other times he is talking, but everything else is so noisy that we can't hear his voice. Either way, we lose the sense of the presence of Jesus meeting with us. And without that, why bother to gather together?

One of the great advantages of a small group meeting in a home is the ability to quiet the distractions, take your time, and welcome the presence of Jesus among us.

Conversation Starters

1. Have you ever been in the presence of someone great, or famous, or really special? How did it feel?
2. What was the most memorable religious service or event you ever attended? What made it special for you?
3. When was the time you most felt God was near?
4. Read again the quote from F. W. Faber. Do you think that is true in your life?

2

Conventional, Institutionalized, Ecclesia

God is Spirit, so those who worship him must worship in spirit and in truth.
— John 4:24

I have either pastored or attended a pretty wide variety of churches. I've worshiped in almost every kind of denominational or non-denominational affiliation. I've been in little country Baptist churches with fifteen people and huge urban African-American Pentecostal churches with ten thousand. I've knelt to the majestic strains of a pipe organ in soaring sanctuaries with stained glass windows, and I've raised my hands and danced to the band in modern auditoriums with no windows at all. I've sung praise with hymns and bluegrass and gospel and American Sign Language. I've worshiped with immigrants from El Salvador and new believers in Turkey. I've pastored large and small churches with diverse memberships, in the country and the city and the suburbs.

All these churches had at least three things in common. All were in a special building. All had one specified person who did most of the talking (when I was a pastor, that was me, though I tried hard to get others involved). And in all of them, the primary role of the people was to sit in rows and listen. To that degree, they were what I call conventional churches.

Conventional Church

Most conventional churches have, in no particular order:

- A special building or meeting place
- Special people called pastors and worship leaders
- A special place up front for the special people, often literally fenced off with a railing
- People sitting in rows trying to look past the backs of other people's heads
- Special "insider" language and practices
- An emphasis on programs, most of which happen in the building

There's nothing intrinsically wrong with any of these things. Conventional churches obviously bless millions of people, or they wouldn't keep coming week after week. A tremendous amount of good is done in local communities and around the world by churches that meet in special buildings and have designated preachers. God called me to spend my career working within that kind of church, and I still believe in it. But a growing number of people, especially in North America and Europe, feel called to something different.

The interesting thing is, there is no place in the Bible that requires special buildings or lectures or sitting in rows. In fact, as far as we can tell, when the first followers of Jesus gathered they didn't have any of those.

Institutionalized Church

The dictionary on my computer defines an institution as "a society or organization founded for a religious, educational, social, or similar purpose." By that definition, all churches are institutions, and there's nothing wrong with that. But when a church goes from serving God and people to expecting people to serve it, it has become what I call "institutionalized." It's sad when that happens to any organization, but it's especially sad when it happens to God's church.

When I talk about "the institutionalized church," here's what I think of. The more of these characteristics that describe any given church or denomination, the more institutionalized it has become.

- An emphasis on the survival of the institution, including frequent appeals for money
- A "we/they" mentality about other churches
- Increasingly bureaucratic church government
- People pushing their own agendas instead of seeking God's direction
- An aversion to trying anything new
- Membership on the books that is much larger than average attendance
- Evangelism as an effort to keep the church going
- Avoidance of church discipline for fear of losing members

This is the kind of church that has given Christianity a bad name, and driven so many away who would otherwise be attracted to the message of Jesus.

Ecclesia

"Church" is the word English translators chose to express the original New Testament Greek word, *ecclesia*. Originally, *ecclesia* could mean any meeting or gathering of people. Greek-speaking Jews used it to refer to those gathered in a synagogue, and the New Testament writers carried it over to those gathered in Christian worship.

When the Bible refers to "the church of [place name]," it does not mean a building where all the Christians in that place came to worship. It was actually rare for them to all meet together at one time. Instead, "the church of [place]" was a collective term for all the Christian believers in that area. Who normally met in dozens of small groups in different homes.

> *The churches here in the province of Asia send greetings in the Lord, as do Aquila and Priscilla and all the others who gather in their home for church meetings.* (1 Corinthians 16:19)

> *Please give my greetings to our brothers and sisters at Laodicea, and to Nympha and the church that meets in her house.* (Colossians 4:15)
>
> *I am writing to Philemon, our beloved co-worker, and to our sister Apphia, and to our fellow soldier Archippus, and to the church that meets in your house.* (Philemon 1:1-2)

So the normal New Testament model for Christian gathering was to meet in someone's home. What did the first Christians do in these house church meetings? Surprisingly, the Bible doesn't really say!

In the Old Testament, every detail of worship in the Tabernacle and Temple was laid out, right down to what the priests were supposed to wear. But when it comes to the New Testament church, about the only description we have is chapters 11-14 of Paul's first letter to the Christians in Corinth. Even there, he is not laying out a specific template for all Christian worship. Instead, he's correcting some particular ways their worship gatherings were being wrongly influenced by their previous pagan religion, or just by their old human nature showing through. Note that he doesn't say anything about how the room was supposed to be arranged, or whether they should kneel or stand or bow when they prayed, or whether a pipe organ is more spiritual than an electric guitar.

Here is how he puts it all together:

> *Well, my brothers and sisters, let's summarize. When you meet together, one will sing, another will teach, another will tell some special revelation God has given, one will speak in tongues, and another will interpret what is said. But everything that is done must strengthen all of you.* (1 Corinthians 14:26)

Everybody participated. Nobody had to do something every time, but anybody could, any time. No one person dominated. No one person orchestrated what happened. As you read on, it becomes clear that there was no pre-set order of songs and teachings and testimonies. People contributed as they felt inspired. Verse 30 even tells the appropriate way to interrupt each other!

It sounds like a recipe for chaos. But as everyone followed common Christian courtesy and focused on strengthening each other's faith, it wound up flowing in peace and order (verse 33).

Of course, the whole reason for Paul writing these chapters is that, for various reasons, sometimes things didn't flow in peace and order. To deal with that, some of his other letters mention elders, deacons, and overseers or bishops who coordinated and looked after the home groups.

Paul appointed some of these for the churches he planted; the Bible doesn't describe how others were chosen. A major part of their job was to make sure the teaching didn't get off track, and that non-Christian practices didn't infiltrate the group (1 Timothy 1:3-7 and 4:1-5; 2 John 1:10-11). One thing is clear: there is no indication that the job description included doing all the talking in the worship services.

These New Testament house churches were not isolated. The Bible mentions several times when they worked together to raise financial support for worthy causes, such as relieving the famine in Jerusalem (Acts 11:27-30; 2 Corinthians 8). The house churches in an area may have all gotten together for special celebrations, such as Easter. And when an apostle or traveling preacher was in town, naturally all the people would want to hear them. In that case they probably pooled their resources to rent a space. Luke describes such a setting:

> *On the first day of the week, we gathered with the local believers to share in the Lord's Supper. Paul was preaching to them, and since he was leaving the next day, he kept talking until midnight. The upstairs room where we met was lighted with many flickering lamps.* (Acts 20:7-8)

Other than these special occasions, when the Christians in the Bible "went to church," here is what happened.

- They met in homes
- They took turns singing and talking about what God was showing them

and doing in their lives
- Everyone was free to share as they felt led
- There was no rigid order of events
- They usually enjoyed a meal, often including the Lord's Supper
- There was coordination and oversight, but no bureaucracy or power structure
- Financial sharing was voluntary, not manipulative
- There was no concept of supporting an institution

Looks a little different from the modern institution too many churches have become, doesn't it? The goal of this book is to help you and a few friends create a modern form of those Biblical *ecclesia* gatherings.

Conversation Starters

1. What is your church or religious background?
2. If you used to attend church but no longer do, how did that happen?
3. Are there any parts of church that you miss?
4. What is the best religious experience you ever had?
5. What parts of Biblical *ecclesia* seem most attractive to you? How might you add some of that to your life?

3

The First Jesus Followers

You will receive power when the Holy Spirit comes upon you. And you will be my witnesses, telling people about me everywhere—in Jerusalem, throughout Judea, in Samaria, and to the ends of the earth. — Acts 1:8

Of the thousands of people who heard Jesus preach and experienced his miracles, only a small remnant stayed faithful after his crucifixion. Just before he went to heaven, the resurrected Jesus told them, *"Now I will send the Holy Spirit, just as my Father promised. But stay here in the city until the Holy Spirit comes and fills you with power from heaven"* (Luke 24:49). In Jerusalem, 120 die-hard followers gathered in a borrowed (or rented) loft to pray and wait.

Fire!

Ten days later, on the morning of the Jewish feast of Pentecost, the Holy Spirit came upon them. By that evening, through Peter's Spirit-filled preaching, three thousand new believers had been added.

Here's how the Bible describes it:

> *On the day of Pentecost all the believers were meeting together in one place. Suddenly, there was a sound from heaven like the roaring of a*

> *mighty windstorm, and it filled the house where they were sitting. Then, what looked like flames or tongues of fire appeared and settled on each of them. And everyone present was filled with the Holy Spirit and began speaking in other languages, as the Holy Spirit gave them this ability.*
>
> *At that time there were devout Jews from every nation living in Jerusalem. When they heard the loud noise, everyone came running, and they were bewildered to hear their own languages being spoken by the believers. They were completely amazed. "How can this be?" they exclaimed. "These people are all from Galilee, and yet we hear them speaking in our own native languages!" . . .*
>
> *Then Peter stepped forward with the eleven other apostles and shouted to the crowd, "Listen carefully, all of you, fellow Jews and residents of Jerusalem! . . . So let everyone in Israel know for certain that God has made this Jesus, whom you crucified, to be both Lord and Messiah!"*
>
> *Peter's words pierced their hearts, and they said to him and to the other apostles, "Brothers, what should we do?"*
>
> *Peter replied, "Each of you must repent of your sins and turn to God, and be baptized in the name of Jesus Christ for the forgiveness of your sins. Then you will receive the gift of the Holy Spirit." . . .*
>
> *Those who believed what Peter said were baptized and added to the church that day—about 3,000 in all.* (Acts 2:1-8, 14, 36-38, 41)

Let's look at this a little more closely. Three thousand people have just had a life-changing religious experience. They witnessed a major miracle: supernatural sound, fire that doesn't burn (did they think of Moses and the burning bush?), and a bunch of men and women from the hills of Galilee praising God in languages from around the world. Then one of them explains it all by saying that the Messiah, the Savior their people have waited for so long, has come! The dreams of their religion have been fulfilled! Three thousand people believe Peter and commit themselves to follow Jesus, and they want to make it public by being baptized.

It takes a long time to baptize three thousand people. By the time they are done, it's getting dark. Supper time has come and gone. But they don't want this day to end. Would you?

So the ones who live nearby invite the others to come home and eat with them. They stay up late talking about what happened. The next morning little groups of them drift back to where it happened, and they find some of the apostles there. They want to learn more, and the apostles start teaching them.

The church is born.

Routine

Over the next few weeks the new believers found themselves settling into a routine. Nobody told them they had to. Nobody sent a plan down from denominational headquarters. They didn't have a heavenly vision of church, or commandments about how it was to be done. What they did have was a new relationship with God and each other through the Holy Spirit – and they loved it. They loved being with God, and they loved being together.

Luke describes what it looked like.

> *All the believers devoted themselves to the apostles' teaching, and to fellowship, and to sharing in meals (including the Lord's Supper), and to prayer. A deep sense of awe came over them all, and the apostles performed many miraculous signs and wonders. And all the believers met together in one place and shared everything they had. They sold their property and possessions and shared the money with those in need. They worshiped together at the Temple each day, met in homes for the Lord's Supper, and shared their meals with great joy and generosity— all the while praising God and enjoying the goodwill of all the people. And each day the Lord added to their fellowship those who were being saved.* (Acts 2:42-47)

Word got out that there were twelve men called apostles, plus a number of other men and women, who had been with Jesus from the beginning. They had seen all the miracles and heard all the sermons, they had spent private time with Jesus, and Jesus had commissioned them to pass it all on. Naturally, people wanted to hear what they had to say. But where could thousands of people all listen at one time?

The answer seemed obvious. The Temple courtyard was large enough, it was meant for religious gatherings, and the big stone wall would reflect a speaker's voice out to the crowd. Many of them were going to the Temple to worship every day anyway. It was perfect.

As they talked about Jesus, many of the apostles' stories were about Jesus' healings and miracles, and how Jesus sent out groups of his followers, two by two, to do the same (Luke 10:1). In fact, most of them were probably there. In a crowd that size there were certainly people who needed healing, so probably when the teaching was done there was a time of praying for the sick, and they got healed.

When it was all over, the crowd broke up into small groups to go home and eat and talk and spend time together. The Bible calls this "fellowship." The next day they did it all again. Other people noticed and asked what was going on. The believers invited them home, and they became a part of it. And the numbers grew.

Through it all, they devoted themselves to prayer. Ceremonial prayers in the temple worship. Healing and miracle prayers as they ministered to one another. Prayers before meals and as part of the Lord's Supper. Prayers of praise and thanksgiving.

And the prayers weren't just talking. Some people never get past, "Now I lay me down to sleep . . . God bless Mommy, God bless Daddy, God bless my dog..." — as if praying is like calling God on the phone and leaving a grocery list on his voice mail. True prayer is a conversation with God. If you're not listening for God's answers in your heart and looking for them in your life, you are missing one of the greatest blessings God wants his children to have.

At least some of the meals included the Lord's Supper. A literal translation in verse 42 above is "breaking bread." Most scholars understand that to refer to the Lord's Supper (or Holy Communion or the Eucharist or the Mass – all different names for the same thing). Verse 46 adds, *and shared their meals* (literally "eating food"). So sometimes they shared the Lord's Supper, and sometimes they just ate. A good old pot-luck may be one of the most New Testament things many conventional churches do!

Community

Luke tells us these first Jesus followers sold their property and possessions and shared with those in need. Jesus didn't require that of everyone who followed him, and we don't see that happening later in the Bible, at least not on any significant scale. This was a special situation. Here's what was happening.

Have you ever been to a resort town where the population balloons during tourist season? Jerusalem was something like that. For five hundred years Jews had been scattered all over the known world. It was the lifelong dream of every observant Jew to visit Jerusalem. Many would save up for years to be able to take the trip. They scheduled it around two of the great Old Testament festivals. The big one was Passover, the remembrance of God delivering their nation from slavery in Egypt. Fifty days later was Pentecost, celebrating when God gave the Law to Moses. The ideal once-in-a-lifetime family trip was to get to Jerusalem in time for Passover, spend the next seven weeks worshiping in the Temple and soaking in the sights and sounds of the Holy Land, and by Pentecost have just enough money left to make it home.

Many of the thousands of new Pentecost believers would have been in this situation, far from home and just about out of money. Just as they were about to leave, they found what they had come hoping for: a fresh experience of God. But even more than that. They were in Jerusalem at the exact time that God fulfilled the centuries-old promise of their faith. The Messiah had come! They experienced the proof!

There was no way they were leaving now. They wanted to stay at least a little longer and be a part of this new thing God was doing. And the ones who lived in Jerusalem wanted them to. So some of the locals sold property and cashed in investments and used the proceeds to support the visitors so they could stay a little longer. After a while most of the pilgrims went back home, where they told their friends and neighbors, and probably worked to repay their Jerusalem hosts. Others may have decided to get jobs and stay in Jerusalem permanently.

And people kept coming to see what was going on. The day of Pentecost wasn't a one-and-done revival meeting. Acts 4:4 says within a few weeks there were five thousand believing men, not counting women and children.

Just like you and me, most of the new believers had jobs and other commitments, so they couldn't keep spending all day listening to the apostles and praying and eating together. But they still got together as much as they could, after work and on the Sabbath (Saturday), and especially on the Lord's Day, which we call Sunday, to celebrate the resurrection. Meeting in homes for worship fit their heritage, because synagogues started as home groups after the Jerusalem Temple was destroyed by the Babylonians. They discussed what the apostles said and what God was doing, they prayed, they shared the Lord's Supper, and they ate and had fun together. Luke's description ends with, *And each day the Lord added to their fellowship those who were being saved.*

Conversation Starters

1. Have you ever been part of a group that experienced something so wonderful you didn't want it to end?
2. What is the closest sense of community you have ever felt with anyone — a college dorm, a military unit, a group on a trip, or something else?
3. What was your most life-changing religious experience?
4. What kind of prayers draw you most into a sense of God's presence and love?

4

How Christianity Spread

The Kingdom of Heaven is like a mustard seed planted in a field. It is the smallest of all seeds, but it becomes the largest of garden plants; it grows into a tree, and birds come and make nests in its branches. — Matthew 13:31–32

When the church was born it was a small Jewish sect concentrated almost exclusively in Jerusalem. Thirty years later it was an international body of Jewish and non-Jewish believers spread throughout the central Roman Empire, with a reputation for turning the world upside down (Acts 17:6). How did that happen?

History indicates that Christianity spread in two ways that sound diametrically opposed to each other: scattering, and attraction. I've discovered that God loves to take things that seem opposite and work them together. Let's take a look at these two.

Scattering

> *A great wave of persecution began that day, sweeping over the church in Jerusalem; and all the believers except the apostles were scattered through the regions of Judea and Samaria . . . But the believers who were scattered preached the Good News about Jesus wherever they went.* (Acts 8:1 and 4)

"That day" is the day Stephen, the first Christian martyr, was killed. Until then almost every Christian in the world lived in Jerusalem. It was the nursery of the new-born church. But the time came when God decided his people had been watching the apostles long enough.

I remember the first time I noticed exactly who went out and started preaching the good news about Jesus. I had just assumed it was the apostles. But look again at verse 1. It was *all the believers except the apostles.* The apostles stayed in Jerusalem. The ordinary Christians, the same ones who ran from the persecution and scattered all over the countryside, were the ones who told everybody about Jesus.

This wasn't a mission trip. They didn't start out to preach. I think it happened something like this. Imagine a Jewish believer named Jon hears that his friend Ike has been thrown in jail for being a Christian. Jon races home, grabs his wife and kids, and runs for the only place he can think of – Uncle Albert's house in Damascus. Jon and family show up at Uncle Albert's front door. Uncle Albert asks to what he owes the pleasure of this unexpected visit. Jon says he's being persecuted for following Jesus. Uncle Albert says, "Who is Jesus?" And Jon and his family tell him.

Ordinary Christians – not apostles, not prophets, not evangelists or pastors or teachers, just plain everyday believers – spread the word of Jesus wherever they found themselves.

> *Philip, for example, went to the city of Samaria and told the people there about the Messiah. Crowds listened intently to Philip because they were eager to hear his message and see the miraculous signs he did. Many evil spirits were cast out, screaming as they left their victims. And many who had been paralyzed or lame were healed. So there was great joy in that city.* (Acts 8:5-8)

There is no indication that Philip was anything other than an ordinary everyday Christian. There was a Philip among the seven chosen to run the food ministry in Acts 6, but that may have been a different Philip — it was not an uncommon name. Even if it was the same person, running a soup kitchen doesn't imply miraculous powers. We do know this is not Philip the apostle, because verse 1 says all the apostles stayed in Jerusalem.

It's extremely unlikely that Philip went to Samaria all by himself. He certainly would have taken his family with him, and probably others came along as well. People fleeing persecution almost always go in groups. Philip was most notable, but we can be sure other ordinary Christians, so ordinary that their names are not even recorded, were doing the same kinds of things.

So how did just-plain-Philip and the others do these miracles? The same way Jesus did: by the power of the Holy Spirit.

Spirit-powered actions are a part of imitating Jesus. Jesus himself promised it twice, before his death and after his resurrection. In John 14:12 he told his followers, *I tell you the truth, anyone who believes in me will do the same works I have done, and even greater works, because I am going to be with the Father.* In Acts 1:8 he told them how it would happen: *You will receive power when the Holy Spirit comes upon you.* A few years later Paul wrote about miracles as a normal part of church life (see 1 Corinthians 12:7-11).

Philip and the other believers didn't set out to do miracles. They were running for their lives. But when people started asking why they had left Jerusalem, they told about Jesus. And a big part of the Jesus story was how he healed the sick; at first in person, and later through the apostles using Jesus's name.

There are sick people everywhere. I'm sure some of those listening said, "Can Jesus heal me, too?" So Philip and the others, probably scared to death, remembered what they had seen the apostles do, and they did the same. And God responded with healings and miracles. *And the disciples* (a word meaning ordinary Christian believers, as opposed to the set-apart apostles) *went everywhere and preached, and the Lord worked through them, confirming what they said by many miraculous signs* (Mark 16:20).

When Philip left Jerusalem he had no idea of planting a church. But miracles can be pretty convincing. *The people believed Philip's message of Good News concerning the Kingdom of God and the name of Jesus Christ. As a result, many men and women were baptized* (Acts 8:12). Suddenly Philip found himself with a bunch of new believers on his hands asking him, "We believe in Jesus, now what do we do?"

Again, Philip did what he had seen the apostles do in Jerusalem. He had already baptized them, when they first believed. Now he started teaching them, and showing them how to imitate Jesus. He was following the steps Jesus laid out in what we have come to call the Great Commission: *Go and make disciples of all the nations, baptizing them in the name of the Father and the Son and the Holy Spirit. Teach these new disciples to obey all the commands I have given you* (Matthew 28:19–20).

When my son John was in college he felt God leading him to visit Cambodia. He found a church in Cambodia on the internet, asked if they would be his local connection, bought a plane ticket, and took off. He thought he would mainly be kind of a Christian tourist, visiting churches, getting a taste of what it's like to follow Jesus in southeast Asia, and sharing a little from his own experience. The Cambodians had a different idea. They thought he had come to teach them more about Jesus and the Christian life, and they wouldn't take no for an answer. So John reached back in his memory to what he had learned from sermons and Sunday School and watching his dad the preacher, and he talked about those things. And God used him.

Philip and the other scattered believers did the same thing. They told people what they had learned from the apostles. When somebody showed interest they taught them more. When you suddenly find yourself taking care of a baby you do whatever you can, whether you feel qualified or not. Spiritual babies should be no different.

Verses 14-25 end this part of the story.

> *When the apostles in Jerusalem heard that the people of Samaria had accepted God's message, they sent Peter and John there. As soon as they arrived, they prayed for these new believers to receive the Holy Spirit. The Holy Spirit had not yet come upon any of them, for they had only been baptized in the name of the Lord Jesus. Then Peter and John laid their hands upon these believers, and they received the Holy Spirit. . . . After testifying and preaching the word of the Lord in Samaria, Peter and John returned to Jerusalem. And they stopped in many Samaritan*

villages along the way to preach the Good News. (Acts 8:14–17, 25)

Philip and company and the new believers were not left on their own. The existing church provided backup as needed. But Peter and John did not stay around and take over. They did not leave a lot of rules and structures. I'm sure they stayed in touch, in case their presence was needed again. But in general, they trusted the Holy Spirit to guide and keep this new group of believers.

Let's recap:

1. Ordinary Christians spread the word of Jesus, wherever they happened to be
2. Ordinary Christians did the works of Jesus, wherever they happened to be
3. Ordinary Christians took care of the resulting new believers
4. The existing church provided teaching and support as needed

We see these four steps clearly in the first half of Acts 8. They repeat in the second half of the chapter as Philip goes to Gaza. We see them again in Acts 9:10-19 with Ananias in Damascus, and again in Acts 11:19-26 with unnamed believers in Phoenicia, Cyprus and Antioch.

In the next years and decades, Christians scattered throughout the Roman Empire and around the world, for all the reasons people move to new places. Wherever they went, the cycle repeated.

Eventually missionary movements and church-planting programs developed as ways of intentionally scattering the seed of the gospel (Acts 1:8; Acts 13). But scattering is only half of the equation.

Attraction

Let's look again at Acts 8:6-8:

Crowds listened intently to Philip because they were eager to hear his message and see the miraculous signs he did. Many evil spirits were cast out, screaming as they left their victims. And many who had been paralyzed or lame were healed. So there was great joy in that city.

Christianity didn't spread just because believers talked about it. People were attracted to what they heard and saw for themselves.

I remember the first time I heard of the Boy Scouts. I was in elementary school. My father had not been a Boy Scout, and I had no older brothers or cousins in the Boy Scouts. An announcement was made in school about an informational meeting. It sounded interesting, so I got my dad to take me to the meeting. I was attracted to what I heard, so I went to a Scout meeting, just to see what it was like. I liked what I saw, and the other boys seemed nice enough, so I joined up. As I continued there were parts I liked and parts I wasn't so crazy about. But in general, I felt that I was getting enough out of the program to continue. Over the years, millions of other boys and girls have been attracted to scouting and similar programs, and the movement has spread around the world.

Christianity spread the same way. Sometimes there was a conscious effort to attract people to church: a dynamic speaker, or some kind of physical help like a medical clinic or a food pantry, or even prayers for miracles and healings. More often, throughout history, it has not been big missionary efforts or evangelistic crusades that attracted people, it has been the lives of believers.

Luke tells us the new believers enjoyed *the goodwill of all the people* (Acts 2:47). As the Holy Spirit worked in their hearts, people could see the results in their lives. In Galatians 5:22-23, Paul lists what they saw: *love, joy, peace, patience, kindness, goodness, faithfulness, gentleness, and self-control.* Those are attractive traits in anyone. These Christians were likable folks.

And they took care of each other. Do you know how Jesus said the world would know we are his followers? Not by the sign on the building we go to once a week. Not by the particular list of behaviors we adopt or condemn. Not by who we allow into our little club. Jesus said, *Your love for one another will prove to the world that you are my disciples* (John 13:35). People could see how Christians cared for each other, and they wanted to be part of that.

In the first few hundred years of the church, there is little record of organized evangelism. In fact, in many places people had to go through a months-long period of training and evaluation before they were even allowed to stay through the whole church service. They not only had to learn the basics of the faith, but prove they were serious by evidence of changed lives. Yet despite periodic waves of persecution under various Roman Emperors, more and more did, and Christianity spread throughout the known world.

This seems incredible to many modern church folks, but it's not just an ancient phenomenon. For the first decades of the Methodist movement, the big Sunday morning worship and preaching service was called a society meeting. There were also small gatherings in homes through the week, called class meetings. These groups focused on in-depth spiritual growth through asking each other questions like, "How is it with your soul?" The only people who were allowed to attend the Sunday morning societies were those who could show a ticket from the previous week's class meeting. In other words, you weren't even allowed to go to church unless you could prove you went to a home group the week before! Yet the Methodist movement showed incredible growth. Even today, many of the strongest churches and denominations are those in which membership is hardest to come by.

To sum it up, ordinary Christians "talked the talk and walked the walk" wherever they happened to scatter. People were attracted by the message, or by stories of answered prayer. As they got to know more about these Christians, they were attracted by other things: their character, their relationships, and the way they took care of each other. The attraction was so strong that people were willing to put up with stringent admission requirements to be part of the group. This is the strong and vital Christian movement that spread the good news of Jesus around the world.

Conversation Starters

1. Part of Philip's demonstration of Christianity in Acts 8 was miraculous signs and healings. Have you ever experienced or witnessed something like that?
2. What groups have you been part of that most demonstrated the kind of character, relationships, and caring described in this chapter?
3. If you found yourself in a place where no one had ever heard of Christianity, and the people asked you to explain it, what would you say and do?

5

How Did Biblical Ecclesia Become Institutionalized Church?

> *They will act religious, but they will reject the power that could make them godly. Stay away from people like that!* — 2 Timothy 3:5

We are often tempted to idealize the early church. It was so vital, so alive, so life-changing! The reality and love and power of God were so manifestly present! It grew and it spread, and it *turned the world upside down* (Acts 17:6, ESV)!

What in the world happened? How did that exciting spiritual dynamo turn into the hide-bound institution so many people find boring and irrelevant today?

People

It has been said that any political or economic philosophy would work fine if people didn't have to be part of it. Human beings seem to have a knack for messing up even the most perfect system. We can certainly see that demonstrated in the church.

Even in New Testament times, church wasn't perfect. Acts 4, describing events that took place within weeks of Pentecost, ends with an idyllic description of the love and sharing among the new Christians. Acts 5 starts with the ominous word, "But. . ."

"But," Ananias and Sapphira decided to lie about their giving so they would look good (Acts 5:1-11). "But," Simon Magus thought the ability to help people receive the power of the Holy Spirit was something he could buy, so he could impress people (Acts 8:18-19). "But," some of the Corinthian church folks were more concerned about filling their bellies at the Lord's Supper than filling their souls (1 Corinthians 11:20-21).

James had to warn against favoritism in the church (James 2:1-4). John had to warn against leaders who wanted to turn the church into their own little dictatorship (3 John 1:9-11). Paul had to warn against those who preached for financial gain (2 Corinthians 2:17).

All this within the lifetimes of many who had seen Jesus in the flesh or been in the crowd at Pentecost!

Looking ahead, Paul warned against self-proclaimed Christians who *will act religious, but they will reject the power that could make them godly.* He added, *Stay away from people like that!* (2 Timothy 3:5).

Politics

For the first several hundred years, these were largely local problems. Then Emperor Constantine stopped persecuting Christianity, and instead embraced it. Suddenly, being known as a Christian leader became an avenue to political power. Over the next few centuries, church and state became intertwined to the point that sometimes it was hard to tell where one left off and the other began. Crusades, the Inquisition, church leaders as heads of states and heads of states as church leaders; it was the ultimate institution.

The problem with institutions is that those who lead them can so easily move from serving the people to expecting people to serve them. This kind of institutionalization is a problem any time – in government, education, medicine – but for the church it is disastrous.

Renewal

Of course, not every local congregation became hopelessly institutionalized. But pastors were trained by The Church, and rituals were prescribed by The Church, and the atmosphere at the top worked its way down. Some people dropped out, or just kept going through the motions if there was a social advantage to it. But others were not content with that. They were not ready to give up on Christianity, and they knew there must be something more to it than their church experience was giving them. Does that sound familiar?

Throughout history, the Holy Spirit has led people to try to regain what they saw in the Bible. They usually began with small groups of people gathering in homes or public spaces, or sometimes hiding in caves or in the woods, praying and talking about God. Almost all of today's Christian denominations started this way, as attempts to renew and reform the institutionalized church of their day. Yet, as with most things involving people, all of them have become more or less institutionalized themselves.

In the 1730s, John Wesley began a renewal movement within the Church of England that became known as Methodism. As we saw earlier, for the first hundred years or so great efforts were made to ensure that the only ones allowed into leadership, or even fellowship, were those who demonstrated "a desire to flee from the wrath to come." But as Methodism developed from a scorned fringe movement to a respectable part of society, people began to come for more worldly reasons. Wesley himself could see it coming. In 1786 he wrote,

> *I am not afraid that the people called Methodists should ever cease to exist either in Europe or America. But I am afraid, lest they should only exist as a dead sect, having the form of religion without the power. And this undoubtedly will be the case unless they hold fast both the doctrine, spirit, and discipline with which they first set out.*

As a Methodist myself, I can tell you from experience that Wesley's fears have been realized in much of his movement.

Institutionalism

Have you ever seen a lava tube? A volcano erupts. Thick, hot molten rock spills over the side in a river that can be dozens of feet deep. As it flows downhill, it begins to cool. The top and the edges start to solidify. The inside is still hot, so it keeps flowing, a little narrower now because the cooled-down outside has peeled off. As it keeps going, the process continues, the white-hot core getting smaller and smaller as the edges harden. Finally, it cools off, too. The result is a long hollow tube of rock: a lava tube. The flaming force of the initial eruption has left just a hardened shell.

Some churches are just institutions planted by other institutions. They may never have had a white-hot core in the first place. But even those that start out hot enough to melt hard hearts can cool. As time goes on and the great days of the beginning become stories told by parents, then grandparents, then church historians, the temperature drops and rigidity rises.

Institutionalism can strike any church, liberal or conservative, modern or traditional, new or old, large or small. Some would even say it's an inevitable consequence of success. In 1789 John Wesley pondered this in what has come to be known as Wesley's Law:

> *Does this not seem (and yet it cannot be!) that Christianity, true scriptural Christianity, has a tendency in process of time to undermine and destroy itself? For wherever true Christianity spreads it must cause diligence and frugality, which, in the natural course of things, must beget riches. And riches naturally beget pride, love of the world, and every temper that is destructive of Christianity.*

A group of people starts meeting in a home to worship God and be with each other. It may only last a short while. Or it may continue for years, with basically the same people. Either of those outcomes is fine; that could be just what God planned for that group.

But sometimes such a gathering really seems to meet a need. That's when Wesley's Law kicks in. Other people are attracted. They outgrow the house and decide to build a building. They decide they want a leader who has been specially educated and can devote full time to them, which means a paid pastor. Suddenly they have debts and financial obligations and big plans stretching years into the future.

All those things can be good. God can inspire churches to make big plans, and God uses people and pastors and buildings to make them happen. We'll talk more about that in Chapter 10.

But as these plans and obligations pile up, they can also create a lot of pressure, especially in succeeding generations. Leaders can gradually start looking at new people as wallets to pay debts and bodies to accomplish plans instead of sinners to be saved and baby Christians to be raised.

When that happens, the church has been institutionalized.

The problem is that when a church is being what it's supposed to be, it attracts people who don't know God. That's a good thing. But it also means you have a church with lots of unbelievers and immature Christians. In many forms of church government, these folks have as much voice in major church decisions as seasoned believers.

Learning God's ways takes time, and being guided by the Holy Spirit instead of worldly wisdom takes a humble willingness to follow God's leading even when it doesn't seem to make sense. Some people, even some Christians, never reach that point. The apostle Paul explicitly blamed these still-immature members for some of the biggest problems in the church.

> *Dear brothers and sisters, when I was with you I couldn't talk to you as I would to spiritual people. I had to talk as though you belonged to this world or as though you were infants in Christ. I had to feed you with milk, not with solid food, because you weren't ready for anything stronger. And you still aren't ready, for you are still controlled by your sinful nature. You are jealous of one another and quarrel with each other. Doesn't that prove you are controlled by your sinful nature? Aren't you living like people of the world? When one of you says, "I am a follower of Paul," and another says, "I follow Apollos," aren't you acting just like people of the world? (1 Corinthians 3:1–4)*

Some Christians never seem to grow up. Others just seem to lose their fire, like the lava tube. Jesus told the church in Ephesus, *I have this complaint against you. You don't love me or each other as you did at first! Look how far you have fallen!* (Revelation 2:4).

But it's not hopeless. His next words tell them how to fix it: *Turn back to me and do the works you did at first.* No doubt some, those who were invested in the institution, ignored him. But the ones who took him seriously started gathering in little groups in their homes to talk and pray and support each other, and *ecclesia*, the real Biblical church, went on.

You can do the same thing today. More and more people are. It's becoming a movement that I and many others believe may be the birth of the next great renewal of God's work in this world.

Conversation Starters

1. What is it about people that makes the generalizations at the beginning this chapter so often true?
2. The first Baron Acton said, "Power tends to corrupt, and absolute power corrupts absolutely." What is it about power that has such a corrupting influence?
3. In your opinion, what in today's church most needs to be renewed?
4. Do institutions have any good points?

II

So What Do We Do Now?

6

Why Should Christians Gather Together?

Where two or three gather together as my followers, I am there among them. — Matthew 18:20

We've looked at why the institutionalized church no longer seems to work for so many Christians. I've more than hinted that at least one answer is for Christians to meet in small groups in their homes. But before we get into what that could look like and how to do it, let's take a step back and ask ourselves, why should Christians meet together at all?

The simple answer is, because the Bible tells us to. God wants us to, and ideally, that should be enough reason for us.

But even though God is our Father, he doesn't just say, "You'll do it because I said so, and that's that!" God likes it when we try to understand why he says and does things. It helps us understand God better, and therefore know and trust and love him more. God doesn't want to leave our curiosity about his reasons frustrated.

To that end I'd like to look at three purposes I believe God had in mind when he called us to meet together, seven things God wants his gathered people to do in order to fulfill those purposes, and twelve reasons they all work best in a group.

Three Purposes

Like any father, God desires a home where he can rest and be himself. Like any father, God desires to raise up children who will be like him. And because God is the ultimate and infinite Father, God desires for his children to bring other people to become part of God's family – ideally, every other person in the world!

These three desires of God show us the three purposes of Christians joining together.

First, Christians join together to create a loving family home where God can rest and be himself. *Now arise, O Lord God, and enter your resting place* (2 Chronicles 6:41). The way we do this is traditionally called worship.

Second, Christians join together to raise God's children to be like their heavenly father. *Imitate God, therefore, in everything you do, because you are his dear children* (Ephesians 5:1). The way we do this is traditionally called discipleship.

Third, Christians join together to equip God's children to bring other people into God's family. *Go and make disciples of all the nations, baptizing them in the name of the Father and the Son and the Holy Spirit* (Matthew 28:19). The way we do this is traditionally called evangelism.

To put it another way, when we gather, our Father wants us to let him know we are happy to be with him, help each other grow up to be like him, and welcome everyone to join us in the journey.

Everything we do as gathered Christians should contribute to fulfilling one or more of these three purposes. Anything that doesn't help advance one of these purposes is an unnecessary drain on time, energy and resources that can hinder our ability to do things of eternal value.

Seven Functions

On the day of Pentecost the church grew from 120 people to over three thousand. In Chapter 2 we looked at Luke's description of their first gatherings to see how the Christian movement grew and spread. Let's look at it again from a slightly different perspective, as a possible model for our own small home gatherings.

> *All the believers devoted themselves to the apostles' teaching, and to fellowship, and to sharing in meals (including the Lord's Supper), and to prayer. A deep sense of awe came over them all, and the apostles performed many miraculous signs and wonders. And all the believers met together in one place and shared everything they had. They sold their property and possessions and shared the money with those in need. They worshiped together at the Temple each day, met in homes for the Lord's Supper, and shared their meals with great joy and generosity—all the while praising God and enjoying the goodwill of all the people. And each day the Lord added to their fellowship those who were being saved.* (Acts 2:42–47)

This is the first description of the early days of the church. The main thing the new believers did, almost instinctively, was gather together. When they did, seven things happened. I call them the seven functions of the church:

1. Worship: praising and honoring God, and offering ourselves to him
2. Fellowship: enjoying and caring for other Christians
3. Discipleship: helping each other grow more like Jesus
4. Evangelism: inviting people into the family of God
5. Service: sharing people's burdens and meeting people's needs
6. Social impact: bringing the values of God's kingdom into our culture
7. Prayer: dialogue with God for closeness, guidance, and help

Each of these is necessary to God's plan for growing individuals and answering Jesus' prayer, "Thy kingdom come, thy will be done, on earth as it is in heaven." Focusing on one or two, like the home Bible study I mentioned in the Introduction, is fine if you are part of a church or other body that provides the rest. If you are not, please don't give in to the temptation to just focus on the parts that come easily. God needs his people doing all seven to fully advance his plan for this world, and we need to be part of all seven to fully grow into what God intends each of us to be.

As we discuss these, I will use the word "church." By now you should understand that I do not mean a building or an institution, but followers of Jesus gathering and working together.

Worship

They worshiped together at the temple each day (verse 46). The first thing most people think of when you mention church is the Sunday morning gathering. Most churches call it the worship service.

Our word "worship" comes from the old English "worth-ship." It means recognizing that someone has worth, that they are worthy. Verse 43 says, *A deep sense of awe came over them all.* People were awestruck by the presence of God. They recognized how worthy he is of worship, of acknowledging his worth-ship.

We see another aspect of worship in verse 47, *all the while praising God.* Worship is praising God's worth, giving praise for who he is and for what he's done.

On a personal level, worship is offering yourself to God. In the Old Testament, that was symbolized by offering animal sacrifices. The animal's life was given in place of the person's life. When you offer yourself to God, you put action to your songs of praise. It's the only appropriate response to the awe God inspires.

Verse 46 says they *met in homes for the Lord's Supper.* The original Greek literally says "for breaking bread." Scholars differ as to whether that specifically refers to the Lord's Supper, includes it along with other meals, or just refers to eating together. Regardless of the meaning in this particular passage, we know from other places in the Bible that the Lord's Supper was an important part of early Christian worship gatherings (see 1 Corinthians 11:20-34).

It's interesting that the one thing many churches consider the most important part of worship is not even mentioned here. I'm talking about music. Music probably was part of the temple worship, but this passage doesn't specifically mention it. That would surprise a lot of people nowadays, because, especially in certain kinds of churches, worship is equated with music. They say, "Oh yeah, we have the worship time with the band and singers, then they sit down and we have the rest of the service."

Worship is much more than music. It's great if your home group has someone who can play the piano or guitar, but it's not necessary. In many places around the world, wonderful worshipful music is made with just a drum to accompany the singing. And some of the most beautiful music you will ever hear is just a blend of human voices or even a solo human voice without accompaniment. So don't say, "My friends and I could maybe have a Bible study or a prayer group, but we can't worship, because none of us are musical." Yes, you can, and we'll talk about how in the next chapter. Music adds to worship, but it's not necessary for it.

Worship keeps us in touch with God. It reminds us of God's love and power. The Bible describes heaven as being full of worship. When we're truly worshiping, not just going through the motions but really entering into worship, we experience a little bit of heaven.

Fellowship

The second goal of Christian groups is fellowship. You may be surprised that I put that so high, right after worship. Is having fun with nice people really a spiritual thing? Well, think about it: the first and great commandment is to love God. What's the second one? Love your neighbor. Then Jesus gave a new commandment to his followers: love each other. "Fellowship" is just another word for loving each other.

If there's one thing many former church-goers miss about their church, it's probably potluck covered-dish dinners. People tend to think the church service on Sunday morning is really important but the potluck dinner is just for fun. But that potluck dinner is important, too. It's fellowship. Most Jesus gatherings include a meal for just that reason.

Having fun eating together with other believers is not a new thing. It dates from the beginning of the church. Verse 46 says, *they shared their meals with great joy and generosity.* In 38 years as a pastor, I've been to a lot of potlucks. I don't think I've ever been to one that didn't have food left over. People find great joy in generosity.

When the big daily worship meeting in the Temple courtyard was over, the Christians broke up into smaller groups and went to people's houses. They were enjoying each other's company. They liked being around people with similar interests and values. If they got hungry, they ate together. That's fellowship.

Of course, fellowship doesn't have to include eating, though somehow it usually does. But Biblical fellowship goes far deeper than just having food and fun together. The original Greek word, *koinonia,* comes from a root that means partner or companion. In the popular phrase of today, it means doing life together. A lot of that is fun, but a lot can be very serious.

One of my favorite Bible stories is when Jesus raised Lazarus from the dead. You can read it in John 11. The climax comes four days after the burial, as Jesus stands at the door of the newly unsealed tomb.

> *Then Jesus shouted, "Lazarus, come out!" And the dead man came out, his hands and feet bound in graveclothes, his face wrapped in a headcloth. Jesus told them, "Unwrap him and let him go!"* (John 11:43–44)

Years ago I heard somebody say something about this I had never seen before. Jesus raised Lazarus from the dead, but when he hobbled out of the tomb, he was still wrapped from head to toe in a burial shroud and smeared with seventy-five pounds of embalming ointment (see John 19:39-40). Jesus left the job of unbinding him and cleaning him up to Lazarus' friends.

In the same way, when people come to new life in Christ, they can still be wrapped up in a lot of their old ways, and smeared with some pretty sticky residue of their old life. An important part of Christian fellowship is helping each other get free of old entanglements, cleaned up from old messes, and healed of old hurts.

Verse 42 says, *all the believers devoted themselves to fellowship.* It wasn't an afterthought; it was vital. They devoted themselves to it.

Discipleship

All the believers devoted themselves to the apostles' teaching (verse 42).

Discipleship is the process of becoming a disciple. A disciple is simply someone who follows the teaching or lifestyle of someone else. If you are a violin teacher who studies and believes in and practices The Suzuki Method of teaching violin, then you are a disciple of Shinichi Suzuki. If in working for social change you study and believe in and follow Martin Luther King, Jr.'s philosophy of nonviolent protest, then you are a disciple of Dr. King. And if you are a Christian who studies and tries to follow and become like Jesus and live according to his teachings and ways, then you are a disciple of Jesus.

A major component of discipleship is teaching, but it's not all academic or intellectual. You can't become like Jesus just by reading a book — even the Bible. You have to do what it says. Christian discipleship is more like an apprenticeship, or coaching. We learn by being around other Christians, watching them and doing things with them as they practice their faith in their daily lives.

Ephesians 4:13 says, *This will continue until we all come to such unity in our faith and knowledge of God's son that we will be mature in the Lord, measuring up to the full and complete standard of Christ.* In other words, until we all become just like Jesus, we can't stop meeting together. Discipleship is how we help each other work toward that goal.

Evangelism

Each day, the Lord added to their fellowship those who were being saved (verse 47).

Most people will acknowledge that there are times and ways they've messed up in their lives. What we don't like to acknowledge is that there is nothing we can do to fix it. Even if we could live perfect lives from now on, it would not erase what we did in the past.

The wonderful good news is that even though we can't fix it, God can. In fact, he already did, when Jesus came to die on the cross in our place, and then rise from the dead to pave the way to heaven. All who choose to follow Jesus are invited to be part of that.

Even better, we're invited to be adopted into God's family. We don't have to pay a price or jump through religious hoops. Jesus already took care of it. All we have to do is follow him into glory.

It's "as simple as ABC." A: Admit you need God. B: Believe in Jesus and what he did for you, and invite him to come into your heart and apply it to your life. C: Commit yourself to stop going your own way and follow the way of Jesus, with God's help. Then just tell God about it in a prayer. When you do, the Holy Spirit of God comes to live in you, and spiritually you are born into God's family and become a new person (2 Corinthians 5:17).

Evangelism is just letting people know that.

What is that important? Because it's the heartbeat of God. God's love is infinite. In Matthew 28:19 Jesus commissioned his followers to *go and make disciples of all the nations, baptizing them in the name of the Father and the Son and the Holy Spirit.* Why? Because *the Lord does not want anyone to be destroyed, but wants everyone to repent* (2 Peter 3:9). God's desire is for every human being to be restored to his family. He wants it so much that he paid the price, at the cost of his own son's life, to make it possible.

> *But how can they call on him to save them unless they believe in him? And how can they believe in him if they have never heard about him? And how can they hear about him unless someone tells them?* (Romans 10:14)

Telling them, evangelism, is the fourth thing every Christian group should aim for, in whatever way God leads each one.

Service

All the believers met together in one place and shared everything they had. They sold their property and possessions and shared the money with those in need (Acts 2:44–45).

The fifth function of God's people is service. I'm not talking about the church service, as in all the religious stuff we do together on Sunday morning. This kind of service is serving other people, helping meet their needs.

Service demonstrates God's love, and it makes us more like Jesus. Jesus said, *Even the Son of Man came not to be served but to serve others and to give his life as a ransom for many* (Mark 10:45). Jesus met people's needs. We become like Jesus by doing the things Jesus did. Your small group of Christians could make a huge difference in somebody's life.

Social impact

This one is not so obvious in the passage above, but stick with me. Verse 47 says the believers enjoyed *the good will of all the people* (verse 47). One of the best ways to generate good will is to make people's lives better. And the best way to improve the lives of a lot of people at once is to make some kind of positive change in society.

Some Christians question whether God really wants us trying to effect change on a societal level. They feel we should focus on saving individuals, and let social change be a side effect of that. Certainly God wants people saved, and certainly saved people make things better. But that doesn't mean we shouldn't work on other levels as well. Many of the Old Testament prophets focused on correcting societal injustice.

Jesus taught us to pray, *Thy kingdom come, thy will be done on earth as it is in heaven* (Matthew 6:10, traditional rendering). God's will is always done in heaven. Where earth is different from heaven, God's will is not being done on earth. That's a call for God's people to act. We should not rest until God's will is being done, and our little part of earth has become more like heaven. That often requires changing society as well as individuals.

For the past two thousand years, the driving force behind what most people consider positive social change has been Christian ideals. The abolition of slavery, women's rights, public education, and reforms in the treatment of criminals and the mentally ill are just some of the areas where Christians have led the way. And there is still a lot of work to be done.

God commanded through the prophet Amos, *Let justice roll down like waters, and righteousness like an ever-flowing stream* (Amos 5:24 NASB). Where a law or a custom or a tradition contributes to injustice or unrighteousness, that law or custom or tradition needs to change. Sometimes this means raising awareness. Sometimes it means supporting certain kinds of legislation. And sometimes it means something more personal. Verse 45 says, *they sold their property and possessions and shared the money with those in need.* Don't you think all those new Christians selling their property and taking care of each other had some kind of social impact? I sure think it did.

To be clear, advancing the Kingdom of God does not mean backing a particular political party or platform. I know good, godly people on both sides of the American political divide. We should know, after all these many years, that we will not bring heaven to earth by legislation and politics.

> *When Joshua was near the town of Jericho, he looked up and saw a man standing in front of him with sword in hand. Joshua went up to him and demanded, "Are you friend or foe?" "Neither one," he replied. "I am the commander of the Lord's army." At this, Joshua fell with his face to the ground in reverence. "I am at your command," Joshua said. "What do you want your servant to do?"* (Joshua 5:13–14)

If this had happened in today's America, Joshua might well have asked, "Are you Republican or Democrat?" The answer would have been the same. And our response should be the same as Joshua's.

Prayer

All the believers devoted themselves to prayer (Acts 2:42).

Prayer is the life-blood of the body of Christ. It should permeate everything else we do, because it is how we hear from God, and it is how we access his help.

If you grew up in a certain kind of church, you may understand prayer as reciting a set of holy-sounding words. Don't get me wrong; written prayers can be really beautiful. If you're not familiar with them, I urge you to check out the *Book of Common Prayer* of the Episcopal Church or the Anglican Church of North America, or a Roman Catholic missal, or the hymnal of any liturgical denomination. Praying those prayers can bring a wonderful blessing. But they are not intended to be the only prayers you pray. They are a guide for your prayers, priming the pump to help you get started.

Other people have the idea that prayer is like calling God on the phone and leaving a wish list on his voice mail. It's cute to hear a four-year-old pray, "Dear God, please bless Mommy and Daddy and the dog and Grandma and Grandpa, and give me a bicycle for Christmas. Amen." But when an adult prays the same way, it's just kind of sad. Unfortunately, a lot of Christians never grow beyond that perception of prayer.

God intended prayer to be so much more. Prayer should be a conversation between you and God. It should be a dialogue: us speaking to God, God speaking to us; God hearing us, us hearing God. The relationship between God and his children is a relationship of love. People who love each other talk to each other and listen to each other. Prayer is how we talk to God, and it's how we hear from God. It's how we get our guidance, our direction, our wisdom. *If you need wisdom, ask our generous God, and he will give it to you. He will not rebuke you for asking* (James 1:5).

Prayer is also how we make requests to God. We ask God to help other people, called intercessory prayer, and we let God know what we need for ourselves.

Some people think God doesn't want us asking him for things. They think it's presumptuous to tell God what we want, unless it's a matter of life and death. They feel like God has more important things to take care of. But you know what? In the phrase of an engineer I know, God has plenty of bandwidth. God has infinite capacity to take care of all the big problems in the world, and your little concerns as well. As a matter of fact, we are commanded to bring our concerns to God in prayer.

> *Don't worry about anything; instead, pray about everything. Tell God what you need, and thank him for all he has done. Then you will experience God's peace, which exceeds anything we can understand. His peace will guard your hearts and minds as you live in Christ Jesus.* (Philippians 4:6–7)

Twelve Reasons

Gathering is a Biblical command

Let us not neglect our meeting together, as some people do, but encourage one another (Hebrews 10:25). Even in New Testament times, some Christians needed to be encouraged to go to church. The writer of Hebrews is not concerned about the fate of an institution, but the health and growth of his readers. Gathering with other believers, even just one or two others, is one of the most important things we can do, for all the reasons we are about to get into. But as we said above, even without all those reasons, the mere fact that God tells us to do it should be enough.

Note that this verse doesn't just apply to weekly church services. What it's really telling us to do is spend time with other Christians. Gathering once a week should probably be a minimum. If the people you spend most of your free time with are not helping you become more like Jesus, perhaps you need to reevaluate.

WHY SHOULD CHRISTIANS GATHER TOGETHER?

There is no such thing in the Bible as a Lone Ranger Christian

Americans are noted for a culture of individuality. We revere the rugged individual, self-sufficient, needing no one. I'm sure there are some good points to that in some situations, but there are some issues with it as well, especially when it comes to living the Christian life. With the exception of a few letters, the Bible was written to communities, not individuals.

One of my pastor friends in Africa posted a meme on Facebook. The picture was of a herd of zebras in the background, and one zebra, that had gotten separated from the group, closer to the camera. The lone zebra was frantically running from a lion who was about to have it for lunch. The caption read, "If 'I'm a Christian but I don't need church' was a picture." (By "church" here, of course, it means other Christians.)

Someone may ask, "But what about hermits?"

It's hard to find a hermit in the Bible. True, God told Elijah to go off by himself and let the ravens feed him, but if you read the whole story, that was just for a short period of time. Elijah wasn't shunning people, he was hiding from Queen Jezebel's assassins.

If you feel like God is calling you to live like a hermit away from everybody, devoting all your time to reading the Bible and praying, I'll allow that possibility. There are a few famous hermits in church history, and it may be that God wants you to do that for a season. But if you're just looking for an excuse to go fishing on Sunday morning instead of go to church, don't talk to me about hermits.

Gathering helps us experience the presence of God

Jesus said, *Where two or three gather together as my followers, I am there among them* (Matthew 18:20). We know that God is always everywhere. As Christians, it's incredibly valuable to train ourselves to be aware of God's presence at all times and in all places. There's a wonderful short Christian book that's been in print for 500 years or more that gives some very practical advice on how to do that. It's called *The Practice of the Presence of God,* by

Brother Lawrence.

But in this verse Jesus is promising something different, a special presence that we may or may not be able to sense, but that is very real. You can probably think of times when you felt God's presence in a special way. Experiencing that is important in ways I can't begin to describe, ways far beyond a feeling of spiritual goosebumps. And Jesus says it happens when we gather with other people.

It is good to be with each other

One of the great biblical pictures of the church is the family of God. Think about the best family gathering you can remember. It may have been Thanksgiving or Christmas, or a birthday or a wedding. As Christians, we are all sisters and brothers, children of our Father in heaven. Whenever we come together, in large groups or small, it should be a joyful and loving family reunion.

There is something special about worshiping with other Christians

The book of Revelations contains some amazing descriptions of worship in heaven, especially in chapters four and seven. None of them describes a solitary worshiper. The smallest number mentioned is the 24 elders around the throne. As we get a wider view, we see that there are myriads, uncounted thousands, worshiping together.

Certainly, we can worship God alone. We don't need musicians and a pastor to worship God; we should always have an individual personal attitude of worship. But in the Bible, worship as an act is almost always corporate. In fact, once Israel settled into the Promised Land, people traveled many days to get to the proper place where they could join others in worship.

Many churches give the impression that worship is led by a pastor or worship leader, performed by the people up front, for the benefit of an audience which is the congregation. Worship does need to be led, but not by the man or woman on the platform. Worship, and human worship leaders, should be led by the Holy Spirit. The worship team is not the folks up front, it's the entire congregation. And the true audience for worship, the one for whom worship is performed and to whom it's directed, is God.

Praying with others multiplies the power

Jesus said in Matthew 18:19, *"If two of you agree here on earth concerning anything you ask, my Father in heaven will do it for you."* Coming together in agreement multiplies the power of prayer far beyond just the addition of voices, in ways beyond our human comprehension.

We can do more together

When it comes to helping people, it's easy to see that a group of people can accomplish more than one individual. Whether it's operating a food pantry or helping somebody move or bringing relief after a natural disaster, our ability to help and serve people multiplies when we're together — and the more of us who are together, the more we can help.

The fruit of the Holy Spirit is relational

I had probably been a pastor at least 25 years before I noticed this. Galatians 5:20-21 says, *The fruit of the Spirit is love, joy, peace, patience, kindness, goodness, faithfulness, gentleness, and self control.* You can't love in isolation; you love another person. Patience and kindness and goodness and gentleness can't exist in a vacuum; you practice them toward other people. We may experience joy and peace and even self-control when we're alone, but we develop them best in response to other people and in sharing them with other people. All of the fruits of the Spirit are ways of relating. We develop them and we demonstrate them by being around other people.

We gather for support

> *Two people are better off than one, for they can help each other succeed. If one person falls, the other can reach out and help. But someone who falls alone is in real trouble. Likewise, two people lying close together can keep each other warm. But how can one be warm alone? A person standing alone can be attacked and defeated, but two can stand back-to-back and conquer. Three are even better, for a triple-braided cord is not easily broken.* (Ecclesiastes 4:9–12)

Peter says the devil is *like a roaring lion seeking someone to devour* (1 Peter 5:8). As we saw earlier, lions never attack an animal from the middle of a herd. They get the stragglers, the outliers, the ones who don't stick with the others. When we stick with each other, we protect each other. We support each other. A youth leader once told me, "Christians are like bananas; separate one from the bunch and it's sure to get peeled."

We gather for accountability

Historically, a signature mark of many revival movements was small groups of people who would meet together for confession and accountability. One would say, "I'm struggling with this" — it might be alcohol or pornography or padding the expense account — "please pray for me." Every week when they came together someone would ask, "How are you doing with that issue? Have you gone to one of those websites you shouldn't go to? Have you had a drink?" Your Jesus gathering is not primarily an accountability group, but it may well develop into that for at least some of you. When you know you're going to be asked by someone who cares, it's amazing how it strengthens your ability to withstand the temptation.

We gather to equip each other

> *Now these are the gifts Christ gave to the church: the apostles, the prophets, the evangelists, and the pastors and teachers. Their responsibility is to equip God's people to do his work, and build up the church, the body of Christ. This will continue until we all come to such unity in our faith and knowledge of God's Son, that we will be mature in the Lord, measuring up to the full and complete standard of Christ.* (Ephesians 4:11-13)

We meet together so the apostles, prophets, evangelists, pastors, and teachers can equip us to do God's work until we all resemble God's Son. As long as any of us don't fully resemble Jesus, we can't stop coming together.

But it's not just the leaders who can equip. Proverbs 27:17 says, *As iron sharpens iron, so a friend sharpens a friend.* The stories of friends on the journey can encourage us, teach us, and sometimes keep us from making the same mistakes they did.

We can also help each other discern when a thought or idea is truly from God versus when it might reflect our own subconscious desires, or even the latest opinion piece we read. Paul addresses this twice in his first letter to the Christians in Corinth.

> *Now our knowledge is partial and incomplete, and even the gift of prophecy reveals only part of the whole picture!* (1 Corinthians 13:9)
> *Let two or three people prophesy, and let the others evaluate what is said* (1 Corinthians 14:29)

We need each other to fill in the gaps in our understanding, and evaluate what we think we are hearing God say.

But "constructive criticism" isn't the only kind of helpful feedback. Some of the times I have felt most encouraged in my life were when someone told me how something I said or did helped them. It seems like God often brings these words just when I need them the most.

We gather to obey "the one-anothers"

If you have a Bible on your phone or computer, take a moment and do a search in it for "one another" or "each other." I think you'll be impressed! The Bible names dozens of different things Christians are to do to or for or with one another. Most of them come from Paul's letters to the churches, but you can find them throughout the Bible. We're told to love each other, care for each other, build each other up, and many more.

It's impossible for a hermit or a "Lone Ranger Christian" to fulfill these Bible commandments. There is not one you can do all by yourself. We have to meet together, or we can't do the "one-anothers."

Groups of Groups

Most of the reasons individual Christians should meet together also apply, at least in part, to groups of Christians working together. Getting more people together on a project can certainly multiply your effectiveness in some areas. If leaders of home churches meet together regularly, they can pray for each other with an understanding few others can have, they can share what is working in their groups and what is not, they can counsel each other on tough issues, and when necessary, they can hold each other accountable. As there are no Lone Ranger Christians in the Bible, there were no Lone Ranger congregations or leaders. Even the Apostle Paul submitted his teachings for the approval of the other church leaders (see Acts 15:1-20 and Galatians 2:1-2).

Being Together Apart

Does meeting together have to mean meeting in person?

Few would disagree that meeting in person is certainly better, if you can do it. If you can shake hands, if you can hug people, if you can hear the tone of voice and see the body language and the look in people's eyes, that's certainly better than sitting in front of a screen. But meeting in person is not always possible. Sometimes there are health or safety issues. Sometimes you're just too far away. In that case, praise the Lord for God's gift of modern technology.

Several years before COVID-19, when free public video conferencing was just beginning, one of our daughters-in-law was going to have her first baby. We had family in five states of the US and a country across the ocean, but we wanted to throw her a baby shower. How did we do it? We had the first online baby shower I ever heard of. It was a little awkward, with time lags and what would now be considered primitive technology, but we felt like we were together. We laughed and talked, and even played a game. We were family together, even though we were thousands of miles apart.

It was a big thing then. Today it's a matter of course. Some Christians are even beginning to meet by virtual reality in the metaverse.

The point is, God is not limited by distance.

> *When Jesus returned to Capernaum, a Roman officer came and pleaded with him, "Lord, my young servant lies in bed, paralyzed and in terrible pain." Jesus said, "I will come and heal him." But the officer said, "Lord, I am not worthy to have you come into my home. Just say the word from where you are, and my servant will be healed." . . . And the young servant was healed that same hour.* (Matthew 8:5–8, 13)

Jesus didn't go into the officer's home. He was in one place and the servant was in another place, many miles away. Yet the servant was healed.

In 1 Corinthians 5:3 the apostle Paul writes, *Even though I am not with you in person, I am with you in the Spirit.* In Colossians 2:5 he writes, *Though I am far away from you, my heart is with you. And I rejoice that you are living as you should and that your faith in Christ is strong.*

This is not the place to speculate about whether what Paul said was just an expression, or some kind of a miraculous metaphysical reality that he experienced. Either way it was real enough that Paul said, essentially, "We're not together physically, but we are together spiritually. Our bodies are apart, but I am with you in spirit." Meeting together online or on the phone or in the metaverse is not the ideal, but it's certainly better than not meeting together at all, and God can work in it.

Feed Each Other's Fire

One of the most common symbols for faith is fire. Usually we picture it as a flame burning in our hearts. But as a veteran of many camping trips, I can tell you it is almost impossible to make a fire with just one stick. It takes tinder, kindling, fuel, and flame to get a fire started, and it takes continual feeding to keep it burning. Pull one stick out of the flames, and soon it will go out. Put it back, and it will reignite.

Each of us is one stick in the campfire. We need each other to keep our faith fire burning.

Conversation Starters

1. Which reasons for Christians gathering together speak most strongly to you?
2. Can you think of any other benefits from Christians meeting together?
3. Which of the "one-anothers" do you have the most trouble with?
4. When did another person or group strengthen your faith or help your Christian life?

7

Here's What It Might Look Like

Well, my brothers and sisters, let's summarize. When you meet together, one will sing, another will teach, another will tell some special revelation God has given, one will speak in tongues, and another will interpret what is said. But everything that is done must strengthen all of you. — 1 Corinthians 14:26

The Essential Elements of a Christian Gathering

1 Corinthians 14 is the clearest description the Bible gives us of a New Testament Christian gathering — what most churches call a worship service. Acts 20:6, 1 Corinthians 16:2, and Jewish synagogue tradition all imply that these meetings happened weekly, if not more often. In verse 26, above, Paul sums it up.

The main point is that everyone present should have the opportunity to be involved as the Spirit leads them. I think Paul would be horrified at the idea that any one person, or even two or three, should do everything while everyone else just sits and watches. Each person should be free to contribute, in a variety of ways.

Let's look at these ways a little more closely.

When you meet together, one will sing. We said earlier that music does not equal worship. You can worship without music, and you can play music without worshipping. Of course, most Christian worship does include music, and it can be a real blessing.

One will sing could mean a solo or a small group that performs music while others listen. God gives musical gifts, as he gives any other kind of gift, to be used for his glory. Those who have the gift praise God by singing or playing. Those whose talents lie elsewhere are helped to praise God as they listen.

One will sing could also refer to a song leader. Psalm 149 begins, *Praise the Lord! Sing to the Lord a new song. Sing his praises in the assembly of the faithful.* There is certainly a place for everyone to sing together.

Notice that this is for everyone, even those who may think they don't have a good voice. The Bible says in several places, *Make a joyful noise* (see Psalms 66, 95, 98, and 100). You may not be able to play an instrument or carry a tune in a bucket, but I bet you can make noise! Just think of the last time your favorite football team scored a touchdown. If you feel uncomfortable singing out loud, consider your discomfort a *sacrifice of praise* (Hebrews 13:15) and sing anyway.

Another will teach. I'm all in favor of formal education. I loved my time obtaining various degrees. But when Jesus said, *Where two or three gather in my name*, he did not add, "and one of them must have a degree from an accredited seminary." Anyone who knows something or has learned something can tell it to somebody else. That's teaching.

Another will tell some special revelation God has given. Encourage people to share what God has been telling or showing them. It doesn't have to be "Thus saith the Lord;" it's more likely to be something like, "I saw a beautiful sunset and I thought about how much God loves to create beauty to share with us."

One will speak in tongues, and another will interpret what is said. If tongues and interpretation are not part of your experience, let's let them go for now. If you are familiar with them, you probably already know how to include them in your worship time.

But everything that is done must strengthen all of you. The Greek verb translated "strengthen" is *oikodomeo*, whose root meaning is to build a house or erect a building. Some translations say *build you up*. The King James

Version renders it *edify*, which comes from the same root as "edifice." That's appropriate, because 1 Peter 2:5 says, *you are living stones that God is building into his spiritual temple.*

A worship service is a spiritual construction project. The living stones are being shaped and put in their place and connected together in such a way that each one can do its job. Everything that happens when we come together should strengthen us all for building up the body of Christ.

One more insight, for which I am indebted to my friend Duane Steward. We've been looking at this verse in the New Living Translation, which renders it in terms of what people will do. In practice this is what happens, and it is an entirely appropriate reading. A more literal translation, however, shows a little different perspective.

> *When you come together, each of you has a hymn, or a word of instruction, a revelation, a tongue or an interpretation. Everything must be done so that the church may be built up* (1 Corinthians 14:26, NIV).

Do you see the difference? Instead of things people do, it talks of what people have, gifts they bring which they can share.

During the week, God put a song on Jenny's heart, or gave Bill a new understanding of a difficult question, and they have those with them when they come. These should be shared. While the meeting is going on, God gives Mary something to say. Now she has it in her mind, and it should be shared.

From this perspective, *everything must be done so that the church may be built up* is not just addressing attitude or motivation. It could also mean that if someone in the group has something God gave them (a song, teaching, or other gift), it must be shared. *Everything must be done.* If something is not done, if anything is not shared, the group will be missing an important piece of building material. It might be that God put it on your heart because he knew someone else needed to hear it.

One of the most important gifts anyone can share is their own story. Encourage people to share theirs, as the Lord leads. It's the best way to get to know each other. And you never know when some part of your story will be just what another person needs to hear.

The perspectives of these two translations, what people have and what people do, are not mutually exclusive. The leader's planned order, the song leader's list of songs, and the speaker's prepared message are all things they have as well as things they will do. The point is that God will often give other members of the group something in addition to these. Make sure there is time and openness in your plan for these to be shared as well, and make sure everyone understands the importance of sharing them.

How It Might Look in Real Life

> *The upstairs room where we met was lighted with many flickering lamps. As Paul spoke on and on, a young man named Eutychus, sitting on the windowsill, became very drowsy. Finally, he fell sound asleep and dropped three stories to his death below.* (Acts 20:8–9)

In 1 Corinthians, we've been looking at Paul's description of an ideal worship service. In these verses from Acts, Luke describes what actually happened in a real one. The room was stuffy, the hour got late, but the preacher just kept talking and talking and talking. (Imagine that!) Finally, one of the young men fell asleep. I wouldn't be surprised if more than one fell asleep, but we know about Eutychus because of the tragic consequences (or almost tragic, because the Lord used Paul to restore Eutychus to life). When they all went back upstairs, Paul picked up where he left off and kept talking until dawn!

I love these verses. They're so real. In fact, I once named a pet cat Eutychus, just because I so identified with the young man.

Your group will be meeting in a real live space. It may be stuffy, or it may be cold. There may not be enough chairs for everyone. Whoever is bringing the message might talk longer than some of the hearers are ready to listen. So now it's time to leave the theoretical and start looking at what a Jesus gathering in your home might really look like.

HERE'S WHAT IT MIGHT LOOK LIKE

A Typical Sequence of Events

Here is one common sequence of events. It's certainly not the only one. I encourage you to pray, discuss, and experiment to see what works best for your group. Some people find confidence and stability in a tested format. If that's you, I hope what follows will meet that need. Others feel bound and constricted by a prescribed way of doing things, and yearn for the freedom to try something new. If you are that person, feel free to use as much or as little of what follows as you like. Ideally, there should be enough structure to make sure nothing important is forgotten, and enough freedom to make sure nothing inspired is quenched. The point is not to check off points on an agenda. The point is to have a meaningful encounter with God.

The way you do things might change each time until you hit on what works for you. Then you'll probably settle into something that is more or less the same every time, at least in terms of the order in which you do things. Try to include all or most of these elements most weeks, even if you change the sequence. God will lead you to what is best for you and your group.

Gathering

You invited people, you told them where and when you'll be meeting, someone has prepared the meeting space, and those who will be playing a specific part in the gathering have made themselves ready. But things really start when people begin to show up.

As people arrive, you naturally fall into some kind of pre-meeting fellowship. People talk about the weather, or catch up on what's been happening in each other's lives. You might have coffee and tea.

I would not encourage having a lot to eat and drink, unless you decided to have a meal together before the gathering. If you meet in different houses each time, it can easily become a competition as to who can put out the fanciest spread. Try not to let that happen. Refreshments, if any, should be very simple. It's really just something for people to do as they wait for things to begin.

Oh, look at the clock! It's time to get started. This is a good time to ask everyone to silence their phones.

If someone you are expecting is running late, you might give them a few minutes, or call to see if they are on their way. Don't wait too long, though. Respect the time and effort of those who made it on time.

Opening

You may choose to indicate the beginning of the service with something symbolic like lighting a candle or placing a small cross on a table, or you may just start. I like to begin by announcing, "Happy Sunday!" If you meet on Sunday, it's a cheerful way to let people know Sunday gatherings are something to celebrate. It also indicates time to stop the side conversations and focus on our purpose together.

If you have any visitors, you've probably already greeted them during the gathering time. It's good to formally welcome them again as you begin, especially if some folks got there late and didn't have a chance to meet them.

As you are welcoming visitors, remember to welcome God — although I hope you don't consider him a visitor!

You may ask, "What do you mean, welcome God? Isn't he here already?"

That's a good point. Yes, God is omnipresent; he is always everywhere. But as we have said, besides God's omnipresence, there is also God's manifest presence.

You may have heard the phrase, "God showed up." The theme verse of this book is Jesus' promise, *Where two or three are gathered together as my followers, I am there among them* (Matthew 18:20). When we gather in the name of Jesus, he is not just there in his omnipresence. He comes in a special way. But God doesn't force a special sense of his presence upon us. He likes to be recognized and invited. Invoking God's presence in this way is why the first prayer of a worship service is often called an "invocation."

Worship

Most groups move now into a time of worship, usually involving music and singing. If you're blessed with a musician who can play the guitar or keyboard or autoharp, that's wonderful, but it's not necessary. Singing *a capella*, without instrumental accompaniment, has a long and distinguished history, and it can be very beautiful. Another option is to sing along with recorded music. You can choose from old hymns, gospel, and modern worship music, in various formats. If you feel adventurous, it's amazing how much a drum of some sort can add, even if there are no other instruments.

One reason many gatherings put a worship time at the beginning of the gathering is because it helps people shift their mental and spiritual focus from whatever they've been thinking about to God. If that is not happening, if people are not becoming more aware of God's presence, then maybe you need to rethink this part of what you are doing.

During this time and throughout the service, stay open to the inspiration and movement of the Holy Spirit. The Spirit of God is what sets Christian gatherings apart from every other kind of meeting. So let him lead! Encourage spontaneous prayers and praises. But don't stop there. Let's look at 1 Corinthians 14:26 again.

> *Well, my brothers and sisters, let's summarize. When you meet together, one will sing, another will teach, another will tell some special revelation God has given, one will speak in tongues, and another will interpret what is said. But everything that is done must strengthen all of you.*

These things can happen anytime throughout the service. If you're not familiar or comfortable with some of these things, that's all right. The important thing is, *Do not stifle the Holy Spirit* (1 Thessalonians 5:19). If you invite God to speak to and through people or move in other ways, and leave space for him to do it, he will!

Praise reports

You've gathered, you've welcomed God and each other, and you've had a time of music and worship. Now is a good time to ask if anyone has any praise reports, often called testimonies. It might be an answered prayer, an exciting thing that happened, or some new insight or awareness of God's presence in their lives. These can be the "special revelation God has given" mentioned earlier. Sharing praise reports and testimonies is important because they build faith. Revelation 12:11 tells us they even defeat the devil!

Sometimes people share spontaneously during the worship time. If they do, that's great. Other folks wait to be asked, and that's fine, too. Encourage people to tell their stories. They are a wonderful way any of you can strengthen all of you.

I do suggest that if someone has something involved to share, ask them to prayerfully prepare it and bring it in the future as the main message. Reserve the testimony time for short, spontaneous sharing.

I have assumed good and exciting things are happening, at least to somebody! If they are not, if nobody is aware of any way that God has moved in their life since you got together last time, that's something you need to work on. God is active in our lives all the time. Help each other recognize that, and build those expectations.

Prayer

We noted earlier that the power of prayer is multiplied when people pray together. One of the advantages of a small number of people gathered in a home, as opposed to a congregation of scores or hundreds of people, is that you can take time for everyone to express their prayers, as well as hear each other's prayers and agree with them. Jesus said in Matthew 18:19, *"If two of you agree here on earth concerning anything you ask, my Father in heaven will do it for you."* It is the agreement that multiplies the power or effectiveness of the prayers.

Allow plenty of time. Expect periods of silence. In fact, encourage them.

That is when people can best sense God's answers, or just soak in his presence.

Some people expect a leader to direct who will pray next. In this kind of small gathering, that is not only not necessary, it can be counterproductive. Let God prompt the prayers. One of our goals in gathering is for everyone to become more attuned to the guidance of the Holy Spirit. Encouraging people to pray as they feel led is a great way to develop that skill.

Many people are very uncomfortable at first with the idea of praying out loud, even in a small group. Encourage them by teaching and example. When I was a pastor I would sometimes even use a little coercion: at the end of a long meeting, I would say, "Somebody please close in prayer." Then I would close my eyes and bow my head and just sit and wait. Eventually someone would pray, if just so they could all go home!

Most likely at first the prayer requests you receive will be for people who are sick or facing medical procedures, or those who will be traveling. These are fine for a start, and there is always a place for those prayers, but try to encourage your people to move on into other kinds of needs, including spiritual and relational. As you grow closer as a group and begin to trust each other, this will become natural.

Discourage people from praying for controversial issues, such as politics. Politically neutral prayers for government and leaders are fine. In fact, the Bible commands us to pray such prayers (see 1 Timothy 2:1-2). However, it's best to leave political issues for personal prayers and private conversations.

As people experience the joy and closeness with God and each other that this kind of group prayer engenders, you may find that the prayer times begin to go so long that they threaten to take over the rest of the service. If that happens occasionally, as the Holy Spirit leads, by all means go for it. But if you find that you regularly don't have time for other, equally important parts of your gathering, it might be better to start a separate meeting, perhaps on a weekday evening, devoted specifically to this kind of prayer. Most likely everyone won't come to that, but those who do will be blessed, and their prayers will be a blessing to the whole group.

Special days

Praise reports and testimonies are often related to holidays and celebrations. This can naturally lead into recognition of special days, like Mother's Day or Memorial Day. If you follow the traditional Christian calendar you may celebrate seasons like Advent and Lent, and days like Pentecost and All Saints Day (to name two of my favorites). All of these can have a teaching value as well as providing the comfort of tradition for those who grew up with them.

Letting a calendar set your themes can feel like a restriction on your freedom. But if you ignore something everyone else is celebrating, it might cause people to wonder. Even if you don't build the whole service around a special day, it may be good to recognize it.

Giving

Now it's time for something you may feel has no place in a home group: giving tithes and offerings.

You might think, "Wait a minute. It's just six or eight of us sitting in a living room. What do we need with tithes and offerings? One of the worst things about churches is they're always asking for money."

Asking for money is one of the things I never liked either, whether I was sitting in a pew or making the appeal as a pastor. But properly understood and properly done, tithes and offerings are not about asking. They're about giving. And developing a generous attitude toward giving is one of the most effective ways we can grow in our faith and Christian maturity.

I'm guessing most of the appeals for money you've heard were based on the idea that your money was needed to advance God's kingdom in some way. It can do that, if used properly, but that's actually just a side effect of giving tithes and offerings. God owns the cattle on a thousand hills (Psalm 50:10). The success of his great plan does not depend on manipulating people into giving money.

Around the world, throughout history and across cultures, offerings and sacrifices of some sort have been an integral part of religion. Usually they are aimed at gaining favor with some supposed diety, or fulfilling some kind of religious requirement. Christians know we don't have to buy God's favor. For us, offering our money symbolizes offering ourselves. And trusting God with your money, and seeing what he does with it, is one of the greatest ways I know to build your faith. That's why I think the offering should have a prominent place in your worship time.[1]

"But if we collect money," you ask, "what are we going to do with it?"

That's a good question. If everyone follows the biblical injunction to tithe, or give 10% of their income, you could wind up with tens of thousands of dollars a year, even in a small group. There may be some small expenses you can use it for, but what about the rest?

This is not a problem, this is an opportunity!

You might use some of your money to fund a service project or outreach. You might use some to work together with other home groups or house churches. You might support a parachurch organization. You might adopt a child through Compassion or a similar charity.

You can even adopt a pastor in another country. Most of the churches in developing countries are much more like the Jesus groups we've been talking about than the institutionalized churches that have stopped working for so many in wealthier countries. I'm in touch with many pastors in Africa, Asia, and the Middle East. Most of them serve churches that are very poor, and usually cannot afford to pay any kind of salary. Yet they do amazing work on the little they have. For the cost of a few sheets of roofing material, congregations construct entire church buildings, using local materials and volunteer labor. With modern communications, you can be in personal online communication with them. Online money transfer makes it very easy and safe to send money, and the pastors can show you exactly what they have used it for. Some may even be able to join in your gatherings by video! Even $25 a month can make a huge difference for an entire church.

Allow me a moment to tell you about my personal favorite cause. Up to

---

[1] The best book I know on this subject, and very readable, is *Trust God with Your Finances*, by Jack Hartman.

80% of African pastors have little or no formal training, leaving 500 million believers without trained pastors. Things are similar in other parts of the world. In 2009 I was invited to Turkey to teach local pastors. They asked for a written summary of what I taught. That became *Pastoring: The Nuts and Bolts*, a 300-page book about how to be a pastor and lead a church. Pastors in Africa and Asia heard about it and started asking for copies, and for permission to translate it. As I write we are printing and distributing thousands of copies free of charge in four languages, with more coming. In some countries $16 can provide ten paperback copies, each of which may be shared by several pastors. Imagine how many lives they will touch! Administrative costs are covered by the directors, so 100% of donations go directly to printing and distribution. For more information, search Doing Christianity, Inc. on Facebook or the web.[2]

God might guide you to help a needy pastor or Doing Christianity, or he might lead you to one of the many other worthwhile projects you can support with the tithes and offerings of your group. The important thing is not to miss the spiritual growth that joyful giving can produce in the givers.

Bible time

The first thing Luke says in his summary of the activities of the first Christians is, *All the believers devoted themselves to the apostles' teaching* (Acts 2:42). The apostles' teaching, of course, is what has been handed down to us in the Bible; Luke is not saying that only apostles can teach! The Bible is God's combination love letter to us and instruction manual for living this life. As the saying goes, "If at first you don't succeed, follow the instructions!" Whether you call it a Bible study, a sermon, a homily, a teaching, or a message, time spent engaging in the word of God needs to be an integral part of what you do.

---

[2] The situation in most developing and Christian-minority countries is very different from North America. There, churches are just being born, following many of the principles outlined in this book. Few churches there have had time to become institutionalized.

Who should lead the study or bring the message? It may be the same person every time, or you could rotate among speakers, setting a schedule a month or two in advance so people can be preparing. You could decide at the end of each meeting who will speak at the next one — this allows for someone to say, "You know, I was having my devotional time, and this scripture really spoke to me. I'd like to share that next week." Or you could wait until you come to message time in your service and then say, "Okay, does anybody have anything from the Lord to share?" Traditional Quaker meetings just enter into a time of silence and wait for someone to feel moved to speak. God can work through all these methods. Maybe you'll do it sometimes one way, sometimes another. That's fine!

In some traditions, the message is preceded by reading one or more passages of scripture. Often these verses are the focus of the message. Other times they are read because a calendar of readings, called a lectionary, says these are the readings for this particular Sunday; the message may relate to all, one, or none of the readings. Don't be too quick to discount this. God often speaks to someone's need through one of these seemingly unrelated bits of his word. Of course, the message should reference the Bible verses it is based on, but often that takes the form of isolated bits of verses. It's appalling to me how many people only ever hear the Bible quoted in disconnected verses. There can be real value in reading a whole Bible story or other logically connected section of Scripture. The word of God is powerful, especially if a meaningful selection is read from a modern translation in a clear and expressive way. Paul advised Timothy, *Until I get there, focus on reading the Scriptures to the church, encouraging the believers, and teaching them* (1 Timothy 4:13).

Preparing and sharing a message from God is a big topic. We'll look at it in more depth in the next chapter.

The Lord's Supper

Following the message is a good time to celebrate the Lord's Supper, also called Holy Communion, the Eucharist, or the mass. Some groups celebrate the Lord's Supper every time they come together, some once a month, and some once a quarter or on special occasions. Some encourage their members to attend a conventional church with an ordained minister to receive Communion. How often you celebrate, who you feel is qualified to preside, and whether children or outsiders can participate largely depends on the tradition most of your group grew up in. All have good reasons for their choices. We'll talk some about who should preside in the next chapter.

What if you're meeting online? When I was conducting online worship services for my denominational church at the beginning of the COVID lockdown, I let people know it was going to be communion Sunday, and to make sure they had a piece of bread or crackers and some grape juice or wine on hand. When the time came, I said the traditional words and prayer online, and everyone ate and drank where they were. If those on the virtual meeting were in a family or other small group, I encouraged them to serve each other. If they were alone, I invited them eat and drink along with me. Again, exactly how you do it will differ according to your tradition or what you are comfortable with.

Some churches include foot washing along with Holy Communion, or as a separate ordinance. If that is your background, or if it sounds interesting, I encourage you to prayerfully consider including it.

Prayers and blessings

You've gathered, you've had some singing and some sharing and someone gave a message. Maybe you celebrated a special event, or shared communion. How do you end?

One of the most important things we as Christians can do is to pray for each other. Everything leading up to this point has built up people's faith and expectations (which are largely the same thing). Don't let that go to waste.

If there are special needs or concerns that were not covered in your earlier prayer time, this is the time to tap that faith.

Perhaps there was something in the message that calls for a response of prayer. This doesn't have to be limited to the old-fashioned "altar call" for sinners to be saved. It could be any kind of need, including praying for each other, other people, or some larger need in the community or nation or world.

Maybe somebody in your group is moving to another city or state, and you want to say a prayer over them. Maybe they're going on a short term mission trip, or going to have a baby or an operation, or they're going away to college. These are special events in the life of your group. Mark them with a time of special prayer and blessing or commissioning.

Touching the one you are praying for can be a very meaningful part of your prayer. The Bible calls it "laying on of hands," and Hebrews 6:2 says it is one of the basic, foundational things every Christian should know. For many people, it just seems natural to put their hand on the shoulder of someone they are praying for. But the Bible also says touch can be a means of imparting or passing on the presence and power of the Holy Spirit (1 Timothy 4:14). If you're not comfortable with touching, don't, and certainly don't try to force other people to. But I encourage you to be open to it. A gentle touch in an appropriate place can really convey a sense of care.

What if you are praying for someone who is not there? Maybe you are meeting on line. Or perhaps someone says, "Would you please pray for my mother? She's in the hospital." You don't have to wait until you can physically go to the hospital. Jesus healed people at a distance (see Matthew 8:5-13). We can pray the same way through the power of the Holy Spirit of Jesus, who is within us and among us as we are gathered in his name. I often lay hands on the person who requested the prayer, in proxy for the one who is not there. It conveys compassion, and it can even increase your faith for healing. Let the Holy Spirit guide you.

Of course, it's not just one specific person who can pray. All of you should pray for each other. *Confess your sins to each other and pray for each other so that you may be healed. The earnest prayer of a righteous person has great power and produces wonderful results* (James 5:16).

Closing

You may want to end with another song, or you may go straight to a closing prayer or benediction, which is the church name for a prayer of blessing at the end of a service. Some use a spontaneous prayer. Others like to quote the blessing God commanded Aaron to speak over the Israelites: *May the Lord bless you and protect you. May the Lord smile on you and be gracious to you. May the Lord show you his favor and give you his peace* (Numbers 6:24–26). There are some wonderful musical versions of this online, in modern as well as traditional styles. And of course, there are other written benediction prayers, and old hymns such as "God Be With You 'Til We Meet Again."

If you are having a meal, you can include a blessing for it in your closing prayer. That way people can move right into eating as soon as they get their food.

Before you close, make sure everybody knows the time and place of the next gathering, and anything that will be happening during the week. Include a reminder to contact people who missed the meeting.

Some Practical Questions

How long should it last?

There are no hard and fast rules as to how long the worship service part of your gathering should last. Plan for 60-90 minutes at first, and see what you settle into. Especially if children are part of your group, don't try to push it too long.

Try to be reasonably consistent in how long you go. It will make it easier for everyone to plan the rest of their day, and people are more likely to invite friends if they feel they can reliably tell them what to expect.

What do we do with the children?

It's easy to plan meetings for adults. It's more difficult when children are involved, especially young ones.

Some groups find it works well to keep the children with them and let them be full participants. Others have children participate in the first part of the service but send them into another room during the message time, so they don't distract the adults. If you decide to do it this way, you may want to have a special interactive children's message before they leave.

I encourage you not to decide too hastily that the children should be sent away. Try having the children participate in the whole service for a few weeks, including encouraging them to ask or answer questions during the message if your format allows for that. For one thing, if the children need supervision, sending them out means an adult misses the message. More importantly, I've heard many stories from proud parents about how children as young as three or four, who seemed to be totally focused on their coloring books or crackers during the message time, later asked a serious question about something they heard in the sermon.

What about the rest of the week?

As your group develops, just meeting once a week for a worship time will not be enough. It's important to encourage everyone to stay in touch through the week, especially with anyone who may have missed the weekly gathering.

Mid-week activities could include Bible studies or prayer meetings, evangelistic outings, service projects, or just getting together for fun. It is best if these can develop as natural outgrowths of your scheduled gatherings.

Everyone doesn't have to be involved in every activity. In fact, many of them can be done best through small groups, or perhaps I should say, even smaller groups. Here's a quote from the smallgroups.com website, which often calls home gatherings "micro churches," in an article called "How to Start a House Church."

If the house church is larger than five or six people, we have found small groups to be very effective. These groups often meet outside of the micro church meeting. When we ask new believers about their favorite part of the micro church meeting, we hear again and again that they enjoy small groups. It is in the context of small groups that new believers open up about their lives and learn to pray with others for the first time. We've also found that gender specific small groups can be very effective. A house church of eight or ten may have one or two small groups of men and one or two small groups of women. Oftentimes, house church leaders meet monthly with the small group leaders for training and encouragement. In fact, small group leaders usually become house church leaders.

But Doesn't the Bible Say...?

Depending on your church background, you group may have to make a decision on topics of worship on which there is not universal agreement among Christians. For instance, should babies be baptized, or only older children and adults? Who can preside at Communion, and should it be wine or grape juice? Are the miraculous gifts of the Holy Spirit for today, or did they die out with Jesus' twelve apostles? Are there limitations on what women can do, or are they on an equal footing with men? People on both sides of these and other questions often begin their arguments with, "The Bible says..."

I have a large tolerance for different interpretations of Bible passages and different ways of doing church. This includes various opinions on how the sacraments should be practiced. However, when I believe the Bible is being misinterpreted to the harm of God's people and his work, I have to speak out. So let me state two things very clearly.

1. The Holy Spirit and his gifts are alive and active in Christians today, and we miss many blessings when we ignore the Bible's repeated command to "eagerly desire" spiritual gifts (see 1 Corinthians 12:31 and 14:1).

2. God used women in leadership in both the Old and New Testaments, and those who would ignore those precedents based on narrow interpretations of two verses miss many blessings if they deny women the opportunity to exercise their gifts in every area of church life.

A discussion of these points is outside the scope of this book. I encourage you to research these questions to the extent that you feel you need to, and then prayerfully do whatever feels comfortable to you and your group. And please don't throw out the rest of this book because of a difference of opinion in one of these areas. Apply 1 Thessalonians 5:21: *Examine all things; hold fast to what is good.*

We have covered a lot in this chapter, but I'm really not trying to make it complicated. In fact, just the opposite: I'm trying to show you that **you can do this**, and give you some ideas if you need them. As long as you are seeking God as best you can through Jesus Christ, by the guidance of the Holy Spirit and according to the Bible, there is no wrong way. God will show you the details that will work best for your specific situation.

Conversation Starters

1. How do you think most people would answer if asked what Christians do when they get together?
2. Have you ever experienced the kind of gathering Paul describes in 1 Corinthians 14:26?
3. What was the setting where you feel you were most "built up" as a Christian?
4. In your experience, what kinds of physical or real-life situations or distractions have made it hard for you to enter into a spirit of worship?
5. Which items listed in this chapter do you feel are essential — in other words, if you don't do them, you feel like you haven't really worshiped or "had church?" Were any essentials left out of the list?
6. How do you feel about the whole idea of tithes and offerings?
7. What does the Lord's Supper really mean to you, not intellectually but in your heart?

8

Don't We Need a Preacher?

He has made us a Kingdom of priests for God his Father. All glory and power to him forever and ever! Amen. — Revelation 1:6

Probably the one thing most people associate with Sunday morning church services is the sermon. It is certainly not the only thing that happens, and it may well not be the most important thing, but most people wouldn't feel like they've been to church without it. In fact, many people refer to their pastor as "the preacher."

As we talk about being God's church in somebody's living room, a natural question arises: "But don't we need a trained pastor for that? Isn't that what you learn in seminary?"

No and yes. Seminary is an extensive, concentrated education in the things that make for a good preacher and church leader, and there is a lot of value to it. But there is nothing in the Bible that says such a course of study is required before someone can lead a group of Christians in worshiping God and growing in faith.

In my New Testament theology class in seminary, I had to write a paper about pastors. I began my research by looking up every verse in the Bible where the word "pastor" is used. Do you know how many verses I found? One. The verse is Ephesians 4:11, and here is what it says: *"Now these are the gifts Christ gave to the church: the apostles, the prophets, the evangelists, and the pastors and teachers."*

That's it — just a title in a list. No definition, no qualifications, nothing specifically about pastors. It does say they, along with others, are a gift to the church, and the next two verses give a joint job description:

> *Their responsibility is to equip God's people to do his work and build up the church, the body of Christ. This will continue until we all come to such unity in our faith and knowledge of God's Son that we will be mature in the Lord, measuring up to the full and complete standard of Christ.* (Ephesians 4:12–13)

The job of the pastor is to work with the other four ministry gifts to equip God's people to do God's work until they resemble God's son. And that's all it says.

You might ask, "But what about the Pastoral Epistles?" That's the name given to Paul's three letters of advice to his proteges, Timothy and Titus. Those letters, and other places in the Bible, have plenty to say about the qualifications and responsibilities of those who would lead God's people. But the word "pastor" does not appear in them.

I still had that paper to write, so I decided to list the main duties most churches expect their pastor to perform: praying, presiding over worship services, preaching, teaching, visiting the sick, counseling, administration, and so on. No matter how small your group is, if you meet together long enough, the need for these things will arise. I found examples of all these in the New Testament church, but I did not find that the Bible requires specific training or education to do them. It doesn't even imply that all those things should be done by one person; in fact, just the opposite. Most institutional churches have educational and other requirements for pastors, and for their purposes they make sense. But the only Biblical requirement for Christian leaders is that they be people of good faith, character, and maturity.

In the minds of most church people, pastors fulfill two main functions: they preach, and in some way they are "in charge." Human nature is such that eventually someone is going to wind up being the one everybody else looks to for guidance and decisions. But it doesn't have to be a seminary trained pastor.

Who's Going to Preach?

You may be thinking, "But if we don't have a pastor, who's going to preach?" The fact is, you may not need anybody to preach, at least in the way that most of us think of preaching. You need somebody to share the word of God, but that doesn't necessarily mean writing a sermon and preaching it from a pulpit. Your group might decide from the beginning that a particular person will bring the message most weeks. If not, I suggest you all take turns, at least until everyone has had a chance to give it a try. As your group goes along, God will work these things out for you, and you will settle on what works best for your group.

Call it a Bible study, a sermon, a message, a homily, a teaching, or something else, this part of your gathering is a time for serious discussion about God, the Bible, and life. As such, it deserves prayerful preparation. This is the part of a home church where most people feel least qualified, so we'll spend a little extra time here, looking at five possibilities for how you can do it.

Broadcast or recorded sermons

There is a wealth of broadcast and recorded sermons available on television, radio, and the internet. I have even put some of my own audio sermon archives online, in a podcast called Doing Christianity. You can watch or listen to one preacher all the time, or a different one every week. You can stick with a style you are familiar with, or experiment with different styles and traditions.

Recorded sermons have several advantages. They are certainly the easiest, if you have a convenient way for everyone to see and hear. With a few exceptions, you can be assured of a solid message. (Steer clear of preachers who push a political agenda, bash other ministries, or seek to make money from their listeners.) And it's a great way to experience different preaching and worship styles.

However, using recorded sermons each week also has some disadvantages. It can seem like you are just watching church instead of having and being church. That can lead to a subconscious attitude of just watching Christianity instead of doing Christianity. Using recorded sermons can make it more difficult to find messages which address what's going on in the lives of your own group. And relying on the professionals to supply you with sermons removes an incentive for all of you to develop the vital skills of reading, understanding, and applying what God is saying to you in the Bible.

Printed sermons

The second possibility is an old one, but it can still be very effective. That is for one of you to read aloud a sermon you found in print, either in a book or online.

You may ask, "If we're going to do that, why not just use a recording? Won't that be more interesting than one of our group reading out loud?" It's true that some people, when they read aloud, can be deadly dull. Usually, this is because of a lack of confidence and a lack of practice. But the advantages far outweigh the disadvantages.

With a live person reading, it is actually easier to pay attention. You can stop and ask questions or have a discussion at any point. There is also a far wider range of sermons available in print than on audio or video, so it's easier to choose one that speaks to the needs and interests and situation of your group. You can benefit from the great preachers of history who lived too early to be recorded. And you don't need an audio system or a big screen everyone can see.

That said, it is important for whoever is reading to give attention to basic factors such as speaking loudly and slowly, enunciating clearly, and putting feeling into the words. In fact, it's not a bad idea for the reader to pretend he or she is their favorite preacher or actor, and try to read the words in the way that person would deliver them. If the reader reads this way, people will be interested, they will listen, and they will benefit from the message.

Bible studies

A variation on reading a printed sermon is leading the group through a published Bible study. There are some excellent ones available in a wide variety of formats, some with video components. They are geared toward small groups, and discussion questions are designed to stimulate interesting conversation and life application. Most are limited to six weeks or so, though some are designed for as long as a year.

The ability to have this kind of personal engagement with God's word to us in the Bible is one of many places where a small home group has an advantage over a large congregation. One possible down side is that most studies assume the group has done some reading prior to coming together, so consider that as you make a decision.

Bible studies usually come in four types: topical, expository, biographical, and doctrinal.

- A topical study will start with a given subject, like marriage or how Christians should handle money, and explore what the Bible has to say about it.
- An expository study takes you verse by verse through a book of the Bible, or perhaps a shorter section like the Sermon on the Mount.
- A biographical study looks at what we can learn from a person or group, such as Mary Magdalene or the twelve apostles.
- A doctrinal study examines the Biblical passages that gave rise to a specific Christian belief or teaching, like the Trinity or the nature of salvation.

If you use Bible studies regularly, it is probably a good idea to switch between different types, to keep things interesting.

Like everything, there is some material out there from fringe groups with questionable teachings, so be careful to choose studies from good authors and reputable publishers. Read reviews and visit the author's and publisher's websites.

With published Bible studies, the leader is simply the person who reads the questions out loud. This is a great place to rotate leadership, so everyone can learn and gain confidence. Of course, you also need someone to keep the conversation on track, and keep things balanced by gently steering the discussion away from those who may dominate the conversation and encouraging those who seem shy. Ideally this should be the leader of the week, but someone else should be ready to step in if needed.

Paraphrased sermons

A time-honored way of delivering a message is for someone to take a sermon prepared by someone else and put it in their own words. In many situations, this may be the best method. In fact, many good pastors commonly re-preach other pastors' sermons.

Paraphrasing a sermon has several advantages over just reading one aloud. You are putting the ideas into your own words, so they sound more natural. You can update illustrations, or use different ones more pertinent to your group. You can emphasize the points you feel are most important for your hearers. And you can build in questions for discussion, if you wish.

If you choose this route, be sure to give credit to the original author. Some feel that once something is printed or made available on the Internet, it becomes public property, and no credit is required. I have even known some pastors who encourage others to use their material and not give credit. However, I have always felt that it is important to identify the original source. If I'm using more than one source, I usually don't give credit unless I'm directly quoting, because that's just called research. But when you are using the same structure and outline and ideas and scriptures and perhaps even illustrations from one particular message, then my feeling is it's only right to acknowledge the original. And I think it increases your hearers' trust in you.

Here is how I would go about it. First, make an outline of what the preacher is saying. Usually, by listening carefully to a video or audio message, you can tell where the heads and subheads are, and the points and the illustrations. Using a printed sermon, this can be much easier done, especially if the author tends to write in a logical sequence. Where the sermon consist mainly of stories, it can be a little more difficult to outline in terms of logical points. In that case, just list the stories. You might write, for instance, "Story 1: [give it a title]: "the point of the story is [fill in the blank]." Then when you paraphrase the sermon you can tell the same story, or you may use a different story that makes the same point. Include the main Scriptures from the original sermon, but feel free to add others as well, and to use a different translation of the Bible if you prefer.

By the way, I mention outlines because they come naturally to me. My first career was in engineering, and I tend to think in a very linear fashion. If you prefer a mind map or a storyboard or some other technique, that's fine. Use whatever method helps you keep track of what the original sermon is saying.

Now go through what you have gathered, and put it in your own language. Many people find it helpful to write everything out word for word. Others feel comfortable speaking from notes or an outline. If writing a complete manuscript would be a chore for you, you don't have to. If it makes it easier, do it. If you do write out a full manuscript, I encourage you not to just read it to your listeners. Make sure it's thoroughly in your head, but deliver your message from notes or an outline, memorized if possible. Especially in a small group, spontaneity and authenticity are much more important than grammar and impressive vocabulary.

Paraphrasing the messages of others has a long history. In fact, John Wesley, the founder of Methodism, required his circuit riders to do this. Very few of them had theological education, so he prepared a set of 53 standard sermons laying out what he felt were the most important things for Christians to hear. His preachers carried them with them as they traveled through the countryside, and memorized Wesley's outline and points. The result was that thousands of people all over Britain and America heard the sermons of the founder of the denomination, in paraphrased form. Today, some very large churches have satellite locations where the leaders of those worship services are required to preach their own versions of the same sermon that the main pastor is preaching at the main campus. If you choose this method of preaching, you'll be in very good company.

Original sermons

The last, and often best, option for your teaching or preaching time is to prepare original messages. This doesn't have to be as scary as it sounds. All it really means is sharing with your friends what you feel God has been telling you in prayer, Bible reading, or in your thoughts. You can share it through a Bible story or passage, something in the news, or something happening in the group or your own life. What makes it a sermon instead of a lecture is that you prayerfully bring God into it — or to put it more accurately, you prayerfully bring out how God is already in it — through appropriate use of the Bible.

Though preaching great sermons can take decades to perfect, getting started is really not as hard as it might seem. If you feel God leading you in this direction, see "Sermons in a Nutshell" in the Appendix.

Is it working?

One of my favorite cartoons shows a pastor standing at the pulpit saying, "This is my fourth sermon on the transforming power of the gospel. Why do you still look like the same old bunch?"

The Bible says the goal of Christians gathering together is that *we all come to such unity in our faith and knowledge of God's Son that we will be mature in the Lord, measuring up to the full and complete standard of Christ* (Ephesians 4:13).

What is *the full and complete standard of Christ?* I think of four things: his character, his actions, his wisdom, and his teachings. Even those who don't follow Jesus usually acknowledge that he was a good, honest, compassionate person. Every children's Bible story book recounts his miracles and healings. The gospels are full of stories where religious leaders tried to trap Jesus, but he was too wise for them. And his last words, as recorded by Matthew, instruct his followers to bring others into God's family and teach them to do and be all these things.

If the format of your teachings is not engaging people with the Bible in such a way that they are growing in all these areas, you need to consider a different way of doing it. The Bible is God's combination love letter and owner's manual for earth and life. But it can't just be read, or even studied. It must be applied to life, and applied to our hearts.

What About the Other Things Pastors Do?

I don't know how many times in 38 years of ministry I've been told that pastors only work one hour a week. Of course, the people who said it were only joking — at least, that's what they said. The truth is, conventional church pastors do much, much more than just preach. In a large congregation, much of their time may be taken up in administrative details that your home group will not have to worry about. But other tasks may arise from time to time in any group of Christians. The important thing to recognize is that these things don't have to be done by a special person called "the pastor." In fact, everyone will benefit if the duties are spread out, and possibly even rotated among the members of your group.

What kinds of things am I talking about? Here's a quick and very incomplete list.

- choosing songs and leading worship
- checking up on absentees
- keeping track of responsibilities for the next meeting
- organizing service or outreach events
- visiting members who are sick or in the hospital
- communicating with other home groups
- giving counsel or advice

None of these has to be done by a seminary-trained pastor. The Bible says we reach maturity by doing the work of the church, not by watching a pastor do it (Ephesians 4:12-13). All these tasks are the work of the church that every member should be encouraged to take part in.

As with preaching, as you go along it will become evident that some of your group are better at some things, and others are better at others. That's fine. God gave each of us different gifts and abilities. The point is, everyone should be encouraged to participate. The entire burden should not fall on one person.

What about the sacraments? Who will perform baptisms when the time comes? Who will preside over the Lord's Supper? At conventional churches, these are the responsibility of the pastor. In many denominations, only ordained clergy are authorized to perform them. I'm sure they had good reasons for making such rules, but I can't find them in the Bible. In fact, I find just the opposite.

Matthew's gospel ends with what is known as the Great Commission.

> *Jesus came and told his disciples, "I have been given all authority in heaven and on earth. Therefore, go and make disciples of all the nations, baptizing them in the name of the Father and the Son and the Holy Spirit. Teach these new disciples to obey all the commands I have given you. And be sure of this: I am with you always, even to the end of the age."* (Matthew 28:18–20)

The injunction to "go and make disciples" is universally understood to be the responsibility of every Christian. Yet the second half of that same sentence says, "baptizing them in the name of the Father and the Son and the Holy Spirit." I don't see how, grammatically or theologically, the first half of that sentence can apply to everyone while the second half applies only to a special class.

As for the Lord's Supper, Acts 2:46 says, *They worshiped together at the Temple each day, met in homes for the Lord's Supper, and shared their meals with great joy and generosity.* In these home gatherings, who presided over the Lord's Supper? We saw in Chapter 3 that in the early days of the church there were many more home groups than there were apostles; more, even, than the 120 followers of Jesus who were present at Pentecost. So who presided over the Lord's Supper? Most of the time it must have been ordinary Christians — often brand new ones.

You may prefer to ask an ordained minister to perform any baptisms.

Your group may be more comfortable receiving Holy Communion at a conventional church service. Those are certainly time-honored options. If you feel led to celebrate these sacraments yourselves, different denominations and groups do them in different ways. I encourage you to make this question a matter of serious prayer and conversation, then follow whatever you sense the Holy Spirit is saying. As long as it honors Jesus and follows the Bible, you'll be alright.

Take Me to Your Leader

One of the first questions the members of your group will be asked when they tell others about it is, "Who is your leader?"

Some people are hesitant to step out and start a home group because they don't feel qualified to lead it, and they don't know anyone who might. Others say, "Who needs a leader? There are only four or five of us. We'll just decide everything together. That whole bureaucratic power trip thing is one of the reasons I stopped going to church!"

That may work very well among yourselves. But when outsiders have questions, I bet you'll find that there is someone in the group whom all the rest of you point to for answers. As a matter of fact, if you are the one who makes the initial phone calls to get the group started, the others will probably think of you in that role.

It's just human nature for some people to defer to others when it comes to questions of organization, administration, or direction. And it's just human nature that others will find themselves taking charge of a discussion, without even thinking about it. Leadership is one of the personality gifts that God gives to some people (Romans 12:6-8). It doesn't make them any better or worse than people with other gifts, but when leadership is needed, it's good that they are there. If you took the initiative to read this book and make some phone calls or have discussions with a few friends, that's a good indication that you have at least some level of leadership abilities. And others will recognize that.

In conventional churches, pastors make a lot of decisions on behalf of the church. In your group, directional decisions, the ones about the purpose and direction of the group, will probably be made by everyone in open discussion. If you have a number of new Christians, it may be that a more mature leadership group will be tasked with making those decisions, instead of putting everything up for a vote among people who may not be ready to take on that responsibility. Operational decisions, details about when and how a certain thing will be done, are usually best left to whoever is in charge of making it happen. Again, none of this requires an ordained pastor.

What if nobody wants to be the leader? That's fine. Nothing says you have to name a leader. As a matter of fact, it's probably a very good thing if nobody is angling for a leadership title. Some people just love to be in charge and tell everybody else what to do, and that's not what a group of friends gathering in Jesus' name needs. Leading a group of Christians should not be a power trip, it should be an expression of serving, often to the point of sacrificing personal desires for the good of the group. When the time comes that someone with leadership skills is needed, God will bring them forth out of your group.

What if you have the opposite problem? At one church I served there were two men with tremendous leadership abilities. They were both wonderful Christians, and in their own way very humble people. Where there was a clear chain of command, they got along fine. But where there wasn't, their natural tendencies to take the lead clashed. At those times it worked best to put them in charge of two different things. If your group is blessed with that kind of a problem, pray for wisdom. God will guide you in how to best take advantage of all their skills. A good place to start is by defining roles and processes, so everyone is clear who is in charge of what.

Leadership skills are important, but they are not the only thing to consider. If your group feels led to designate a leader, look for solid evidence of Christian character and maturity (see 1 Timothy 3:1-13 and Titus 1:6-9).

Conversation Starters

1. What do you think about the five different sources of messages mentioned: recorded, printed, Bible studies, paraphrased, and original?
2. If you were asked to bring the message or sermon one week, how would you feel, and what would you do?
3. Which of the other pastoral functions would you feel comfortable doing, and which ones would you not want to be responsible for?
4. In the context of a home Jesus gathering, what does "leader" mean to you?

9

How to Start

> *Do not despise these small beginnings, for the Lord rejoices to see the work begin.*
> — Zechariah 4:10

You're still reading. That means you feel like there is at least a good chance that God wants you to give this idea of two or three gathering in Jesus's name a try. What exactly do you need to do to make it happen?

Before You Begin

As with most things in life, your chances of success will depend largely on your preparation. I've broken that down into eight steps. For the sake of clarity, I've listed them as discrete actions. In practice there will be a lot of overlap.

Pray

No matter what you are doing, things will go best if you start with prayer. You need to be as sure as you can that this is God's work you are doing, and you are doing it God's way. *Unless the Lord builds a house, the work of the builders is wasted. Unless the Lord protects a city, guarding it with sentries will do no good* (Psalm 127:1).

You might tell God, "Lord, you know it seems like church has stopped working for me recently. But I've been reading this book about Jesus gatherings. Are you asking me to do something about this? Please guide me."

Then listen for an answer. It probably won't come in words you can quote. God usually communicates through our spirits. Don't be too quick to discount "something told me" or "I had a feeling." Often that can be God answering your prayer for direction.

Is starting a Jesus fellowship something you normally would have thought of on your own? If not, that might be a good sign that God put the idea in your head. I often pray this way: "Lord, it seems like this might be something you want me to do. If I'm wrong, please make it clear. Otherwise, I'm going to go ahead and step out in faith."

Research

You have already started the research process by reading this book. That's good! But don't stop there. Search out answers to every question you can think of. Then look for questions you didn't think of. As with any kind of research, you don't need to know everything, but you should at least have an idea of how much you don't know. And you want to know enough not to embarrass yourself!

A great place to begin is on the internet. You might start with a search for books and websites using keywords like "house church," "Bible study tools," and "free online pastor training."

I'm sure I don't have to tell you to be careful about what you find online. Look for websites that post a statement of faith that fits with the Bible and looks similar to other sites you trust. Avoid sites that attack people or ministries or seem only to want your money.

The best kind of research is personal experience. Look for a house church you could visit. Your search on "house church" may have brought up a way to find some. If there is not one close by, make the drive anyway; this is not for every week, it's just research. Visit as many as you can. You may find you love everything about one. More likely, you'll find much to like, and a few things you would do differently. At the least, you'll make some connections to people you can call for advice and support for your own group, and that can be invaluable. And if you find one you love close by, maybe you should just join it! It could be that God's whole purpose for you reading this book was to make that connection.

In Chapter 6 we talked about the value of working with other groups and leaders. Every Christian needs other knowledgeable, mature, compassionate Christians to bounce things off of and hold us accountable. This is especially true of those who are in any kind of leadership. This research phase might be a good time to identify those you would feel comfortable with. They may well be leaders of other house churches, but don't automatically discount pastors, active or retired, or even seminary professors. There are those who would love to support a house church ministry with their theological and ecclesiastical ("how church works") knowledge. Some may even have tried to initiate such a ministry, but their congregation or denominational leadership wouldn't go along. I know — it happened to me!

Talk it over

It's important to broach the idea of a Jesus gathering with someone you trust, like your husband or wife or a good friend. At this point you don't need a detailed plan or a decision to go forward. This conversation will probably go more along the lines of, "I've been feeling this way and I ran across this idea. Do you think I'm crazy?"

Don't choose someone whose automatic answer will be, "Yes, you're crazy." On the other hand, "Do what you want, I don't care," is also not helpful. Find someone who will be understanding and supportive of the feelings that have brought you to be thinking about this. If you are normally hesitant about new things, you need a person who will encourage you to at least consider it a little more. If you are the kind of person who easily gets excited and wants to jump into every new idea, you need a person who will gently tether you to reality. Remember, *plans go wrong for lack of advice; many advisers bring success* (Proverbs 15:22).

From this point on in this book, when I say "you," it could mean you as an individual, or it could mean you and whoever you are talking and working with in this possible adventure. Probably, the more often you can take it the second way, the better off you will be.

Pray again

Tell God about what you learned in your research, and the conversations you have had. Sure, God already knows it — he was there. But as you bring it before God, he will help you clarify it in your own mind. If you listen carefully, you'll probably even notice that he adds his own comments, or at least nudges your thoughts in a certain direction.

The Bible says, *Never stop praying* (1 Thessalonians 5:17). There is no such thing as too much prayer.

Count the cost

Now it's time for a reality check. Jesus said in Luke 14:28, *Don't begin until you count the cost. For who would begin construction of a building without first calculating the cost to see if there is enough money to finish it?* (Luke 14:28).

You might think, "It's just having a few friends over every week. I do that all the time. What kind of cost could there be?" A commitment like this will cost you some time. It will cost you some effort. If you decide to have it in your home and serve everybody coffee, it will cost you the price of the coffee.

One thing many people don't consider is what's called "opportunity cost." If you decide to spend every Sunday morning (or whenever you decide to meet) doing this, you give up the opportunity to do whatever other things you could do with that time, like continuing to try out other churches or forms of worship in person or online, or traveling over the weekend, or even sleeping in or watching a football game.

If you decide to try forming a Jesus gathering, it will definitely cost you a step of faith. It won't be the proverbial "blind leap of faith," because you won't be blind. You'll be prepared and you'll be prayed up. But it costs something to overcome your fear and step outside of your comfort zone.

Name names

You have prayed and researched and talked it over with someone you trust. You have prayed some more, you've taken a good hard look at what this might cost you, and you still think this might be something God is calling you to do. Now is the time to ask God to bring to your mind some people who might be interested in joining with you in this adventure. Of course, from the first time you started thinking about the possibility of a Jesus gathering, you have probably had some people in the back of your mind. Now it is time to take the concrete step of making a list.

This is a big step. Before it was all speculative. Now you are shifting from dreaming to planning. Putting names on paper (or pixels, as the case may be) signals to your mind, "Wow, I might actually be serious about this!"

Start with people you're pretty sure feel the same way you do: Christians who are disaffected with institutionalized church, but have not turned off on the whole idea of Christianity, and miss worshiping and fellowshiping with other Christians. As you prayerfully start your list, people will come to mind. Some you've already been thinking of. Others will seem reasonable after a little thought. One or two unexpected names may pop into your head. I encourage you not to just dismiss those people out of hand. It could well be God answering your prayer. After all, you've been asking God to guide you.

This initial list doesn't need to be long, and you can always add to it later. What you are really doing here is getting names down on paper so that you can look at it and tell yourself, "Wow, I guess there actually might be two or three — or more! — people who would be interested."

Present the idea

Now comes another big step: mention the idea to some of the people on your list. Some may not be interested, but I bet some of them will. You don't need many to start; in fact, you don't want too many. If it's just the one or two friends you mentioned it to earlier, that's fine. Call it your "what if" group.

Get together and talk about the idea in your house or a coffee shop or even by video chat. Greet each other and catch up, maybe start with a prayer, and then discuss the idea. When you are done, you might just realize that this little meeting was essentially the thing we've been talking about all along: two or three gathering in Jesus name. And you enjoyed it!

Go or no-go?

It's crunch time. Are you going to try making this happen, or not?

Maybe you decide this is really not for you. You gave it a try, and your best discernment is that this is not what God has called you to after all. If that's the case, that's fine. You have been seeking God's guidance, and this seems to be it. Certainly don't do anything that you don't feel God is leading you to. At the least, you've learned something, and you had a nice get together with some friends. And you know a little more about how to pray for God's work in the world.

But we're going to assume that you decide to go for it, or at least take the next step. So what's that?

Plan Your Trial Run

It's time to make detailed plans for your first gathering. Don't make these plans on your own. Ask your "what if" group to become a planning group.

I recommend that you explicitly call this a pilot or trial run. That way neither you nor your friends feel like they are obligated to some kind of open ended commitment. As a matter of fact, even when you have your official launch, you may want to say, "We're going to try this for six weeks, then we'll stop and have an evaluation to decide if we want to keep on going." People are much more likely to commit to something for six weeks than for an indefinite period. For now, we are focusing just on your first trial gathering.

As you plan the order in which you will do things, consider the flow. Does one element naturally lead into the next, or is there something jarring or distracting? It's kind of like feng shui applied to events instead of furniture. For instance, if you've just finished a beautiful worship song and everyone is feeling peaceful and focused and ready to hear from God, that's not the time to announce that the neighbors have asked people not to park in front of their driveway.

Your trial run invite list

For this first meeting, you want to make sure that the people who come are likely to be supportive and encouraging. There may be some on your list whom you think are good possibilities once you get going, but may not be the best people to be there at this first, experimental meeting. God will guide you.

Just like you, everyone in your planning group probably has some people in the back of their minds they think would be good for this Jesus gathering. Share your lists and discuss them. This is not a time for gossip, but it is a time for everyone to be agreed on the right people to begin this experiment. For that reason, everyone should have veto power. In other words, if anyone is not comfortable about a particular person, don't invite them for this trial phase. After all, you are not looking for large numbers. You are looking for a small group who are really interested in meeting with Jesus. For this pilot time you need people you can count on for that to be their focus.

Limit your list to no more than twelve people total. More than that and you will lose the kind of close interactions that make these home gatherings so special. If anyone will be bringing children, whether you count them in the twelve-person limit depends on their ages and how you see them being involved.

The time before the time

People will start arriving, finding a place to sit, and making small talk while they wait for things to start. Don't leave this time to chance. Often people decide before a function even begins whether they are going to come back.

Try to have your trial run at the same time and place as you plan to have your regular gatherings. It will help you see how well the plans you made will actually work. Will parking be an issue? If you plan coffee or finger food, will the layout of the space accommodate that? Where will everyone sit? Will they be able to see and hear each other? Will anyone be bringing children? If so, will any special provisions be necessary for them?

The time

It's good to plan out how you see the time progressing. Will you have a designated sequence of events? Will you try to hold those events to a certain amount of time? Or is your ideal that everything be spontaneous, under the guidance of the Holy Spirit? Even if that is your plan, I recommend that, at least for your first meeting, you make a list of the essential elements that you want to make sure happen. I have discovered that the Holy Spirit can inspire people as they make plans just as surely as he can inspire people in the moment.

One of you will have the responsibility, formally or informally, of guiding how the meeting moves; for instance, recognizing that there are no more prayer requests to share and it's time to move into another song, or whatever comes next. This doesn't have to be the same person each time. But for each gathering, somebody has to say, "OK, it's time to get started." You need a designated person who moves the meeting along, transitions between one section of the meeting and the next, and gently calls the group back to focus if they begin to go astray.

As you plan your first gathering, here are some things you will need to decide:

- Will your worship include music? If so, how will that be done? Who will be in charge of it?
- Who will bring the message or Bible study? Will there be a passage of scripture read in association with it? If so, who will read that?
- When and how will you share praise reports and testimonies? Who will lead that time?
- Will you celebrate holy communion, or any other kind of special recognition?
- Will you receive an offering? Or, for this first meeting, will you just talk about the concept? If so, when and how will you do that?
- When will you have a time of prayer, and who will lead it?
- How will you close?

You probably won't want to create a written bulletin or order of worship to hand out to everyone (although you certainly can if you want to), but it's important to prayerfully think out beforehand the basic things you want to include and the order in which they should happen. That way those who will be in charge of different parts of the meeting will have an idea when to be ready. And it's helpful to have a list so the leader doesn't forget something. Even after I had been pastoring for 20 or 30 years, it was not uncommon for me to accidentally skip an element of the service. (Most often the thing I forgot was the offering, which didn't make the finance committee very happy!) So a written order of worship is a good back up, even if no one sees it but you.

On the other hand, make sure you leave room for the Holy Spirit to move. I don't mean a line in your order of worship that says, "Between the second song and the message we leave thirty seconds to see if God wants to do anything." Paul advised the Christians in Greece, *Do not stifle the Holy Spirit* (1 Thessalonians 5:19). Consciously try to sense God's guidance. If you feels the Spirit is guiding you to do something differently than you had planned — for instance, an extended time of focused prayer instead of the next song in your list — have the faith and confidence to say so.

As the group matures, everyone should learn to be open to that kind of guidance, not just a designated leader. Encourage people to feel free to say, "I feel like maybe God is saying we should do such and such." One of the great advantages of the small group setting is that everyone understands that you are all growing in this together. If someone says they feel like God is saying you should pray more instead of moving into another song, most of the time you should go along. It doesn't matter a whole lot whether they were actually hearing from God, or it was just their own idea. The point is the learning process.

Just don't argue about it — "God told me we should sing!" "No, God told me we should pray!" If that happens, what God is really telling you is to just be humble and follow the leader!

The time after the time

People won't magically disappear when you say your final amen. It's as important to plan this time as it is to plan the time before things start.

Figure out how you will make sure everyone knows when and where the next gathering will be. If you are going to have a meal after the fellowship, decide if you will say grace as part of the closing prayer, or after everyone has their food. Plan who will be responsible for the food, the drinks, the cleanup, and all the other details that go into a group of people eating together. Don't forget to make sure that whoever is hosting the gathering has a large enough table or other accommodations for everyone to eat comfortably.

If it's football season, figure out what you'll do if someone wants to turn on the game. Will that be a planned part of your after-worship activities? Or will you let people know ahead of time if that is not part of the expectation? Try to anticipate what people might want to do, and be prepared.

Finally, decide whether you want to plan any kind of mid-week follow up, either for evaluation or as a pilot for a possible regular mid-week gathering.

Trial run checklist

- Pray, and enlist prayer support
- List the people to invite
- Arrange a place
- Decide on a time
- Figure out how you will evaluate the trial run and decide whether to move forward
- Make a plan, including the pre- and post- times
- Invite the people on your list, and get responses if possible
- From the people you expect to be there, decide who you will ask to do what
- As the time approaches, send reminders
- Keep on praying!

You can do all this yourself, but I recommend you enlist your "what-if" group to help. They will feel invested, and it will give you a break. Allow plenty of time. A lot of it can be done via email or texting, if that is more convenient for you, but at least one in-person get-together is probably a good idea.

Launch Your Trial Run

You have prayed, you have invited people, and they have said they will come. You have planned it and imagined it in your head. Finally the time has come. What might it look like?

Since this whole thing was your idea, let's assume you offered to have the first gathering at your place. You cleaned house and got everything ready. Your what-if group came early for prayers and moral support. The time is drawing near for the first guests to come. You're a little bit nervous. Will anyone actually show up?

The doorbell rings. Somebody came!

You open the door, say hello, and thank them for coming. You take their coat, and food if they brought some for later. You offer some coffee or tea and catch up or make small talk.

A few more people come. You introduce any who don't know each other. Everyone is a little uneasy, not quite sure what to expect. But as you go on, you begin to feel like maybe this is going to work after all.

Your announced starting time arrives. I recommend that you make a practice of starting right on time, unless you actually see someone walking up your sidewalk. There are some people who, if they know you won't start until they get there, will seem to get there later and later each week.

You start into your plan. Some things go smoothly and some are a little awkward. Some people are happy to talk, some are hesitant to talk, and perhaps some are a little bit suspicious: "What did I get myself into?" But as you keep going, you put each other at ease. By the time you reach the final blessing, everyone kind of looks around and thinks, "That wasn't bad. It was kind of nice."

Evaluate Your Trial Run

We'll assume you follow the worship time with a meal, which everyone enjoys. This is a natural time to raise the question of whether people think this was something they would like to do again. In fact, if you don't raise the question, someone else probably will.

There are three possible answers to that question. If it was obvious that everyone thinks it was a disaster, the answer is no. But that's extremely unlikely. It may be that some really enjoyed it, and others felt like it was nice, but not their cup of tea. That's fine, and perhaps it would not be reasonable to expect everyone to say they loved it. In the case of a mixed response like that, get a feel for how many would like to return, and take this into account as your what-if group has its evaluation. In that case, the answer to, "Are we doing this again next week?" is, "We'll talk and pray about it, and let you know." The third possibility, and the one I believe is by far most likely, is that almost everyone will say they really enjoyed it and would like to do it again. In that case, the answer is, "Of course!"

Finally, after some help with the dishes, everyone leaves. Perhaps the members of your what-if group hang around a bit to talk about how things went, or maybe you do that in the next day or two. If there's any chance that you will be wanting to meet again next week, don't wait too long for an evaluation, in case there are changes you need to let people know about.

Let's assume that you decide, "Yeah, this wasn't perfect. There were some awkward moments. But we can probably fix those. All in all, we think it's worth trying again."

A Few Meetings In

You decide to give it six weeks. After three or four times, things are beginning to run much more smoothly. You greet each other with hugs. You've begun to settle into a routine. People feel like they know what to expect.

You're more comfortable with what you're doing about music and the message. People are beginning to be more open about sharing prayer requests and what God has been doing in their lives. You're beginning to connect with each other through the week, formally or informally. If somebody doesn't show up, one or more of you checks to find out if they are okay. In fact, things are beginning to really hum along!

At this point, it's still likely that just two or three of you are basically doing all the work. This is a good time to really encourage others to take on something. You can make a general announcement calling for volunteers if you like, but it usually works better to personally ask specific people to do specific things. These can be tasks you or others are already doing, or something new. Tell them you believe they are the right person for the job, and offer to help them get started.

Your Jesus gathering has become something you look forward to. Imagine church being fun! There will still be some changes. There is always room for improvement. But it's reaching the place where people are beginning to think about inviting their friends. If it keeps going like this, you'll have to read the next chapter!

Conversation Starters

1. Have you talked about this idea with anyone yet? If not, who will it be? (Perhaps that's a silly question — presumably you're discussing these conversation starters with someone besides yourself!)
2. How could you go about finding a house church to visit?
3. What knowledgeable, mature Christians might you ask to be your theological and ecclesiastical back-up?
4. Who might you invite to be in your what-if group?

10

What If It Really Takes Off?

And each day the Lord added to their fellowship those who were being saved. — Acts 2:47

As we come to the close, I want to talk about something many people never think of. What if everything seems to go right?

Six Months from Now

Imagine it's six months from now. You and a couple of friends decided to start getting together in your living room to meet with Jesus. You quickly felt comfortable with each other. You enjoyed the fellowship. Maybe one week you all prayed together about something, and the next week, the person who asked you to pray couldn't wait to share how God answered. You thought, "Wow! There really is something to this praying together as a group." Or somebody shared a story or message, and someone else said, "Thank you. I really needed to hear that." Oh, sure, there were a few minor bumps and adjustments, maybe some people even stopped coming, but all in all, things went great.

As you got a few weeks in, you discovered that one or two of you really enjoy sharing messages from the Bible. You started off with everyone rotating responsibility for the message, but as you went along, a couple of you really seemed to have a gift in that area. The same thing happened with the worship time. You found that one of you was a pretty good musician. She enjoyed leading the singing, and the rest of you enjoyed singing along.

Whenever group members called each other during the week, or ran into them in the neighborhood, the conversation quickly turned to something about your last gathering — and it was almost always a good thing.

Most importantly, you began to experience the promise of Matthew 18:20, *Where two or three gather together as my followers, I am there among them.* You were aware of that special presence. You all realized that you were looking forward to your weekly gatherings. You really missed them if you had to be absent.

In fact, your group was beginning to look a lot like the description of the first Christian gatherings we read about in Chapter 3.

> *All the believers devoted themselves to the apostles' teaching, and to fellowship, and to sharing in meals (including the Lord's Supper), and to prayer, . . . [They] met in homes for the Lord's Supper, and shared their meals with great joy and generosity— all the while praising God.* (Acts 2:42, 46-47)

Some of your group were enjoying things so much that they started inviting friends to come along. One was a friend from a former church who had also stopped attending. Another was someone who had shared their frustrations about the institutionalized church. Another overheard two of you talking together and asked about it, so you invited them to visit.

To your surprise, some of them took you up on your invitation to try it out. Some came once and didn't come back, but others did — and they kept coming. Then they started inviting their friends. Your fellowship started growing. *And each day the Lord added to their fellowship those who were being saved* (Acts 2:47). Just like Bible times!

As God brings new people, he is bringing new skills — maybe another musician, or a good speaker or organizer. When the time seems right, ask them to get involved. It will cement them into the group, and give you options for times your regular musician or speaker is unable to come.

As this happens, you will find that you quickly reach the place where you have enough people to really get involved in service and outreach. This is very important in growing to become like Jesus. Jesus said, *Even the Son of Man came not to be served but to serve* (Mark 10:45). We grow as Christians as we serve and help each other. As you are looking for more ways to spend time together, why not do things that help other people?

There are all kinds of small service projects that you can do as a group. You can rake leaves for an elderly neighbor. You can tutor at the local school. You can volunteer at a food bank. You can help build a house with Habitat for Humanity. The possibilities are endless, just in the area where you are.

An unexpected side benefit of doing service projects and helping people in need is that even more people will be drawn to your group. One reason so many people have become disillusioned with institutionalized churches is the perception that they are more interested in maintaining their institution than in helping people.[3] When they see your group doing the things they know Christians ought to do, they will want to know more. Some of them might start coming, too. And the growth goes on.

What If We Grow Too Much?

Let's say at the beginning you were meeting at a different person's home each week. As more people came, you outgrew some of the smaller homes. Then you outgrew the medium-sized ones. You are about to outgrow the biggest space you have. Now what do you do?

First, you praise the Lord. You have discovered five very important things.

1. You can meet with Jesus without sitting in pews, listening to a pastor and looking at the backs of other people's heads.

---

[3] In my experience, most churches do help people; they are just not very good at letting it be known.

2. You can be the church and have church, just you and your friends.
3. When two or three of you gather together as followers of Jesus, he keeps his promise to be there among you.
4. There are more people than you realized who are just like you. They want to meet with God, but for them, the institutionalized church has stopped working.
5. You are obviously meeting a need in people's hearts. You are helping people grow closer to God!

These are great things to discover. Praise the Lord for them!

But you have also discovered one more thing: if you keep on doing what you have been doing, you will soon no longer have a place to do it in! You will have outgrown the biggest place you have. You will be completely out of room to meet.

Sound familiar? You are repeating exactly how the early church grew. You have reached the attraction phase we talked about in Chapter 3. You don't have to go out looking for new people. They are automatically attracted by what they see in you.

What do you do now? The same thing you always do: ask God for his guidance. To help you discern God's answer for your group, here are four ways you could logically go.

Option 1: Do nothing

Your first option is to do nothing. Don't make any plans, don't make any changes, just keep doing what you have been doing and see what happens. I don't recommend this, but when you are listing options it's always good to explicitly include the option of not doing anything. That will cause you to consciously consider what will happen if you procrastinate, kick the can down the road, or just pretend there is not a problem. Scarlet O'Hara famously said, "I'll think about that tomorrow." The problem is, it is happening today!

What are the pros and cons of not changing anything about what you have been doing in your meetings with Jesus?

On the plus side, doing nothing is certainly easiest. There's no work, no thought, no concern about offending anyone who likes things the way they are. And while you are doing nothing, you can tell yourself that you really are doing something. You can say you are praying, or waiting for a sign, or researching, or whatever. Of course, you do need to do a reasonable amount of that. But it can become an excuse not to make a decision.

What's the down side? Well, let's think it through. If people know there's no more room, they will stop inviting their friends. Feeling that you can't invite your friends will change the spirit of your group. If the spirit of the group changes, some of your number, even long-time members, may become frustrated and stop coming, because it's no longer the group they loved. Even in an online meeting, there is a big difference in the interpersonal dynamics of a group of twelve versus a group of thirty or a hundred. There will come a point when some who loved the intimacy of the small group you started with will feel you have outgrown them, and they may look for something else.

It is very hard to hold a status quo. Most things in life are kind of like roller skating uphill: either you are moving forward or you are slipping backward. It's very hard to stand still. But lots of people try!

So you could just not do anything and see what will happen. I'll tell you right now, what will happen will not make you happy. Inaction is rarely a good option. But it's one that many people choose because it's so easy.

Option 2: Cap your growth

A second possibility is that your group decides not to accept any more people. You say, "This is it. We've reached our maximum size, and we're going to stop here." As in the first option, you are trying to maintain the status quo. The difference is, this time it's a deliberate decision.

A growth cap shares three positives with the first option. It promises to maintain your group, it's easy, and you don't have to make any other decisions.

The reasons against are also similar to those of the first option. They just become obvious faster. Some of your group may see this, and disagree with the decision so strongly that they stop coming themselves. Wow, that seems like a drastic step! Why would someone be that dead set against keeping a good thing going? Because they can see that it won't keep it going. If you make a deliberate decision to turn people away, it will kill the spirit of your group.

Again, let's think it through. You are in this position because your group has been growing. People are saying, "I've heard about what happens in your group. I've seen the excitement in my friends who come to it. I want to know God like that. Can I come?"

With option two, your answer is, "Nope. Sorry. Good luck finding a place." It's like the tea party scene in Alice in Wonderland: a new person shows up, and everyone shouts, "No room! No room!"

A decision to turn people away ignores one of the main reasons God invented the church in the first place, which is to invite more people into his family. It makes your group's comfort level more important than the spiritual needs of other people. It makes your convenience greater than the Great Commission. In other words, it's beginning to sound an awful lot like some of the worst aspects of an institutionalized church — just what you created your group to avoid.

But never fear! You do have two other options that I think are both very good.

Option 3: Move out of the living room

The third option is to find a larger place to meet. If you have outgrown the biggest space you have, but you don't believe God wants you to stop growing, then you need to get another space.

Often school buildings or theaters are available for rent. If you are willing to change your meeting time, you may find a local church who will let you rent space in their building. In rare cases it may even be possible to buy or build your own building. A separate space can be a great tool for ministry, if it is used properly. Just make sure it stays a tool for ministry and doesn't become the focus of your group's existence.

At this point it's time to face what may feel like a shock. You have been meeting in homes because church has stopped working for you. If you move into another space, people will start to think of your group as a church. Of course, any gathering of Christians is a gathering of the church, in its true meaning. But if you decide to keep growing beyond what you can fit into somebody's home, you have basically decided to become a church in the conventional sense of the word.

Before you decide to skip the rest of this section and move on to the fourth option, there are some good things to be said for conventional churches. And since you are doing this yourself, maybe you can avoid the institutional parts that made other churches stop working for you.

First, moving into a bigger space means you can accommodate more people. You can keep inviting your friends, and the excitement of the change means even more might come. More people means more ability to do good things.

Second, you can attract different people. While most people are more comfortable in a living room than in a church service, there are some who feel the other way, and this will be more attractive to them.

Third, you can hire someone to do what you can't. If you keep on growing, you will find that there is more to do than your volunteers can handle, either for lack of time or lack of training. But that's alright, because growth means you will be able to hire a pastor, at least part-time. Your new pastor will have training and education that probably nobody in your group has. And a paid pastor will be able to devote more time to the ministry than any of you volunteers.

Finally, the decision to transition from a home fellowship to a more conventional church opens up a whole new future. Many vibrant and healthy churches started as home groups. Sometimes the transition was the plan from the beginning; home gatherings were just the first step in a planned church plant. But many churches started exactly as we're talking about here — perhaps most churches throughout history. Two or three people started to gather as followers of Jesus, his presence combined with their faithfulness caused the group to grow, they felt led to find a bigger place to meet, and they grew into a church. Even though your experience may not reflect it, a conventional church, done right, really can be a very good thing.

Of course, there are some points against the decision to grow that direction.

The first is that almost always, a place to meet will cost money. Paying a monthly rent may be a difficulty for the limited number of people who have been fitting into your living room, even with the overcrowding.

Second, while growth means more people to do good things, it also means more people to take care of. Depending on how available and equipped your people are to visit folks in hospitals and help each other out and do counseling and resolve conflicts, you may get to the point where it gets beyond the ability of your volunteers.

Third, as a worship space implies a church, a church implies a pastor. And with the pastoral care duties, preaching, administration, and other responsibilities that come with more people, you may find that you have to hire one. We have looked at the good points of hiring a pastor, and I'm all in favor of them, but there are two down sides to hiring a pastor that you should be aware of. One, of course, is the monetary cost. Not only can that be a big consideration, but the need to hire a pastor often comes at the same time as the need to hire a meeting space, so you suddenly have two new and substantial financial commitments. The other potential problem is that if you hire a pastor people will be tempted to say, "Well, now we're paying the pastor to do this" — visit the sick, or bring the message, or organize an outreach — "so I don't need to do it." People stop doing the work of the church, which is one of their most important means of spiritual growth (Ephesians 4:11-13).

Finally, in a larger space the first impulse is to arrange chairs in straight rows. Psychologically, that works against group participation, and makes it very difficult to maintain the closeness and family feel of the small group you started with. If your meeting space allows, arranging chairs in an arc or semi-circle can help with this, while still allowing a focus on an a speaker or song leader, communion table, or screen.

As we said, many vibrant and healthy churches started as home gatherings, and it may be God's plan for your group. If you believe that is where God is leading you, ask him to guide you with specific decisions and plans. Ask him to put you in contact with the right people, and to give you favor with them. Ask God to provide the resources you need. Pray for wisdom as you face new decisions and update plans.[4]

I strongly encourage you to seek out other churches that started as home groups, and learn what you can from them. Develop relationships with pastors and churches in the area. Consider joining one of the many voluntary associations of churches that work together. You may, to your surprise, even feel led to look into joining a denomination. I know you are reading this because church stopped working for you. But I have served as a denominational pastor for 38 years, and there is a lot to be said for being part of a good established denomination or association. Some of them are doing great work. And there are many good Christians faithfully sitting in denominational pews who badly need someone like you and your group to help them find the way forward.

A larger space is a third option for when you outgrow the living room, and often a very good one. But there is one more that, for many groups, may be even better.

Option 4: Spiritual mitosis

The last option is what I call spiritual mitosis. Mitosis is the biological process by which one cell divides into two daughter cells. It's the normal way in which our bodies grow. The apostle Paul wouldn't have known that when he called the church "the body of Christ," but the Holy Spirit who inspired his writing did. If mitosis is the way God designed for physical bodies to grow, we should look for a spiritual parallel for spiritual growth.

To put it another way, your fourth option is to multiply by dividing. Instead of trying to all stay crowded together, solve your space problem by sending some of your members to plant a new group. If you turn one group into two,

---

[4] My book, *Pastoring: the Nuts and Bolts*, goes into much greater depth about the issues and opportunities that may arise as you move out of the living room, with options and best practices on how to become an effective, and hopefully non-institutionalized, conventional church.

you have multiplied yourselves by 100%.

Most people have an immediate negative reaction to the idea of dividing their group, for obvious reasons. We'll get to that in a moment as we look at the cons part of the pros and cons. But there is a very big upside to spiritual mitosis. Let's look at that right now.

Basically, the positives of multiplying by dividing are all the positives of what you already have. The reason is, you are not changing what you've been doing. You already know how to do it, and you do it well. Spiritual mitosis is your best opportunity to continue that. It actually gives you the best chance of accomplishing what the first two options seem to promise. Spiritual mitosis retains all the advantages of two or three gathering in the name of Jesus that we've been talking about throughout this book. But there are additional advantages as well.

Adding another group makes you much more flexible. Different groups can meet at different times and in different neighborhoods to meet the needs of more people. If several of your people live over on the other side of town, you can locate your new group closer to them. If you have current or potential members who work Sunday mornings, the new meeting can happen at a time that is more convenient for them.

Starting a new group will make you develop new leaders. This is not a problem, it's a good thing. It's amazing to watch how God uncovers the leadership gifts he has placed in people when the need arises. As I see more and more of my friends retiring, I can tell you, the body of Christ always needs new leaders.

Sending half your people to start a new group is almost like going back in time to when you started. If you approach it right, there is a new excitement, a fresh sense that God is doing something. And the smaller numbers will allow a return to the closeness that had started to become difficult as more and more people came to your original group.

Neuroscientists have discovered that our brains work differently with different size groups. We relate one way to groups of three or less. A brain change happens when more people show up. We relate to people in groups from twelve to thirty differently than we relate to people in groups from one to three, or four to twelve. When you started out with three or four people it was easy to feel close to each other. As you grew that closeness and vulnerability became harder. Once your group passed twelve or fifteen members, your relationships changed. Re-forming as two smaller groups can bring back the closeness that was part of what everybody liked so much in the beginning.

Let me mention one more great advantage to spiritual mitosis: there is little to no financial cost! You'll still be meeting at somebody's home, you'll still be taking turns bringing coffee and snacks, and all the work will still be done by members of the group. Only now, there will be two groups of people being blessed and blessing others.

All in all, spiritual mitosis, multiplying into new groups, is the only option that allows you to continue what has been working so well for you, and share it with all the new people who want to get involved.

Now I will be honest with you, there are two things that will make this option a tough one to carry out.

The big one, of course, is that you have built up some really close relationships, and now you will no longer be meeting every week with some of those people. This is the main reason so many groups fail to even consider this avenue. But you aren't moving a thousand miles away! You still live in the same place. You can still see each other as often as you want to. And now, you have the chance to build the same kind of close relationships with a new group of people.

The second hurdle you will have to get over is that if the new group is going to have a good chance, you will be sending some of your best and most qualified people to get it started. Not only will you miss their fellowship, you'll miss their talents, too. If you still only have one musician, or one person who has been bringing the message every week, then one of the groups will be left without those skills, at least at the beginning.

Let me strongly urge you: unless God specifically leads you otherwise, send your one musician or teacher to the new group. Their presence might be vital to its success. Your present group has developed the strength to continue until God raises up replacements. And if the Holy Spirit is leading you this way, it's amazing to see how God will provide. God will raise up people to fill the places of those whom you send out to start the new group. These new leaders will be blessed by discovering and using their gifts, you will be blessed by what they bring, and the body of Christ will be blessed by however God uses them in the future. In fact, that's how God did it in the New Testament.

> *Among the prophets and teachers of the church at Antioch of Syria were Barnabas, Simeon (called "the black man"), Lucius (from Cyrene), Manaen (the childhood companion of King Herod Antipas), and Saul. One day as these men were worshiping the Lord and fasting, the Holy Spirit said, "Appoint Barnabas and Saul for the special work to which I have called them." So after more fasting and prayer, the men laid their hands on them and sent them on their way.* (Acts 13:1–3)

Saul later changed his name to Paul, and wrote most of the New Testament letters.

Who were the best and most qualified leaders in the Antioch church? Paul and Barnabas. Who did the Holy Spirit call to leave that church to plant others? Paul and Barnabas. But the Antioch church didn't fall apart. It thrived, under new leaders God raised up, for centuries. Your group could do the same!

How to Multiply by Dividing

As with everything, soak the whole process in prayer. Ask God for wisdom about how to broach the subject with the other members of your group, and how to answer questions and objections. Once you decide to proceed, you will all need God's wisdom. Seek God's guidance about new locations, times, and all the other details. Be prayerfully sensitive so that no one's feelings are hurt unnecessarily, especially those who may be opposed to the move.

Look for another Jesus gathering or home group that has successfully multiplied itself, and talk with them about their experience. They will probably be able to give you some great advice. But remember that their group is not your group, and their experience may not be yours. Take from them what seems to fit your situation, but don't feel obligated to do everything just the way they did.

The big question, of course, is who will start the new group, and who will stay with your current group. Should you let people divide themselves up, or make a strategic plan? Should you cut your numbers right down the middle? Should you divide according to who lives where, or those for whom different meeting times or days work better? Or should you send out just a small group of leaders to start the new group, expecting it to grow as your original gathering did?

It could well be a combination of all these. If you have two musicians who are each capable of leading worship, or two people who are good at bringing the message, it seems like a no-brainer to keep one in the original gathering and send the other with the new group. But just because it seems like a no-brainer doesn't mean you shouldn't pray about it. God might have a surprise up his sleeve. As you pray, God will guide you about how to do these things. He will help you figure it out.

Once you have decided who continues your present work and who starts the new adventure, let the new group make the decisions about where and when they will meet and how it will work. If you, as the founder of the current group, are not one who will be starting the new one, it will be tempting to "help them out" by telling them what you think they should do. Unless God specifically guides you to say something, resist this temptation. Let them make their own choices, even their own mistakes. It's the only way they can develop their own leadership skills.

Now the only thing left to do is set a date and send them out. Don't just say, "It's been fun, good luck!" Make it meaningful. This is a significant passage in the life of your group, and it's something to celebrate.

I recommend you make your last regular meeting together a commissioning service. Keep the mood positive. Don't let people see it as a split or a loss, or cry, "Oh no, what are we going to do without this person who is leaving to be with the other group?" Celebrate it as a new birth. Celebrate it as multiplication. Celebrate it as a time of new opportunities. Include a meal if you can. Keep the atmosphere positive, but not necessarily light. Certainly include a solemn time of praying over each other.

As we said, your friends are not moving thousands of miles away. The leaders should meet regularly to maintain contact and coordination, and perhaps for some kind of oversight. And it is important that the groups get together every now and then. You could have a joint worship service in a rented space; there is power as more people unite in worship. Or have a picnic, or work on a project together. Old friends need to maintain fellowship, new folks need to meet each other.

I used to tell my congregations, "God is up to something. He has gathered this group of people, at this place, at this time, for a reason." I say that to you as well. God is up to something with you. He led you to read this book. He has you thinking about friends who might be interested in starting a Jesus fellowship with you. He gathered you and them at this time and your place for a reason. I think it's exciting!

Conversation Starters

1. What would you say are the signs of a successful home fellowship?
2. What would you consider the ideal size? What would be too big?
3. If you had a committed group of six to twelve Christians, what activities might you do?
4. Which of the four options seems best to you? Can you think of any others?
5. Have you ever been part of a group or business that sent people out to start a new group or open a new location? If so, what can you learn from that experience?

Epilogue: You Can Do This!

You read this book because, for whatever reason, church has stopped working for you, or it never did. You love God and think of yourself as a Christian. You know there must be others who feel the same way. You want the fun and blessings of fellowship with other Christians, the power and joy of worshiping with other Christians, the peace and comfort of praying with other Christians, the discipleship and spiritual growth and maturity that comes of talking and studying and learning with other Christians, and the sense of fulfillment that comes of serving people with other Christians. These are all good and wonderful things that no one can do all alone, no matter how spiritual they are. And you can't believe that the only way to experience these things is to carry all the baggage of the institutionalized church.

You say, "Yes, that all sounds wonderful, but the idea of starting a group is still scary." And it is.

Maybe you feel unqualified. I would encourage you, if that's the case, go back and re-read Chapter 8. We asked, "Don't we need a preacher?" and the answer was no, at least not in the sense that most people think of preachers. Jesus said, *Where two or three gather as my followers.* He didn't say, "as long as at least one of them is a preacher." Just two or three people. Two or three scared people, two or three untrained people, two or three seemingly unqualified people, it doesn't matter. If you gather as Jesus' followers, he is there with you.

The devil would love nothing better than to frighten you into not trying. But the Bible says, *God has not given us a spirit of fear and timidity, but of power, love, and self-discipline* (2 Timothy 1:7). So let me encourage you: God is up to something. He led you to read this book for a reason.

Jeremiah 29:11 says, *"I know the plans I have for you,"* says the Lord. *"They are plans for good and not for disaster, to give you a future and a hope."* Paul wrote in Philippians 4:13, *I can do everything through Christ, who gives me strength.*

God has good plans for you, and you can carry them out through Christ, who will give you the strength to get it done.[5]

As we finish, may I ask you a favor? If you found this book helpful, please leave a review on Amazon, or wherever you found your copy. It's amazing what a difference that can make in helping others who might need this book find it. If you could do that now before you forget, or put it on your task list, I'd really appreciate it.

I'd like to close with one of my favorite quotes, from John Ortberg: "If you want to walk on water, you have to get out of the boat."

I believe in you. God believes in you. You picked up this book because you want more of God. That makes God happy. You read all the way through because, I believe, God wants you to at least consider having church and being church the way it happened in the New Testament. It is the way probably more Christians have had church and been the church throughout history and around the world than any other way. It is a way that is still happening around the world. And it is a way that will work for you when the institutionalized church has stopped working.

You and God can do this. As God told Joshua, *This is my command. Be strong and courageous. Do not be afraid or discouraged. For the Lord your God is with you wherever you go* (Joshua 1:9).

---

[5] If you are a real Bible stickler, and I hope you are, you will recognize that the context of both of those verses is a little different than what we have been talking about. Context is very important. But I do believe that God uses Bible passages to encourage us in situations other than the specific context the authors were writing about. The principles that applied to their situations can also apply to ours.

Appendix 1: Sermons in a Nutshell

Shelves of books have been written about how to prepare and preach a sermon. If you are interested, I encourage you to read some of those. However, they are all aimed at professional pastors preaching in conventional churches. For a more condensed treatment that may be more applicable to your situation, there is a chapter on preaching in my book *Pastoring: The Nuts and Bolts*. Here I'll condense it even more, and just address the most basic points you will need as a non-professional bringing a message to a small group of friends in your living room.

Let me stress again that you don't need to write original sermons. Any of the five methods of bringing God's word and the apostles' teaching will work fine. But I do believe preparing original sermons is the best way to bring God's specific message for your group. And it is one of the best ways to grow in your own knowledge and understanding of the Bible.

Every sermon should do three things: explain, apply, and encourage. In other words, help your hearers understand the Bible passage or topic or situation you are talking about, give them something concrete to do about it, and urge them to do it. This may seem obvious, but I have heard sermons that gave fiery calls to get out of the pews and do something without a clear idea of what to do or why to do it. I have heard sermons called "How to Do X" without a clear explanation of why X is something I should want to do, and no encouragement to get started. And I have heard sermons (and unfortunately preached some myself) that clearly explained the meaning of a Bible passage and stopped there, leaving it for the hearers to figure out what to do and motivate themselves to do it. You need all three steps if you want your message to make a difference in people's lives.

Don't try to put too much into one message. In seminary I was told, "Preach about two things: preach about the Bible, and preach about twenty minutes." The time can vary, of course, depending on your tradition. But whatever your time goal, don't try to cram more into it than your hearers can process. Explain clearly, illustrate abundantly, and spread your points over multiple messages if need be.

Finally, and this may sound strange coming from someone who for 38 years made his living by preaching, but whatever you do, don't be preachy. You know what I mean. People won't listen long if you seem rigid, legalistic, or judgmental. *Speak the truth in love* (Ephesians 4:15).

How to Understand the Bible

Many people have the impression that the Bible is very difficult to understand, its meaning only accessible with special training. Sometimes that is because the preachers they have heard like to show off their education with big words and technical jargon. But I think one of the biggest reasons people think the Bible is harder to understand than other books is because they read the Bible differently than other books. Oddly enough, this can be more true of Christians than non-Christians.

Think about it. How do most Christians read the Bible? An unfortunately large number rarely do. They only turn to the Bible in a time of loss or crisis. Then they open it at random, hoping God will mercifully take them to the verse they need despite their lack of study in the past. What other book do you read like that?

More serious Christians may follow a daily devotional. Most of these quote something from one part of the Bible one day, give some inspirational comments, then the next day go to a completely different part of the Bible. This is a big improvement, because at least it's every day, but it is still not a normal way to read a book.

The best way is to follow a plan that takes you through the whole Bible. These can be front-to-back, chronological, or in sections. But even those who follow a systematic Bible reading plan often spend less time in their Bible every day than they do in their novels or magazines. Many of what we call the books of the Bible would just be short chapters in most of the books we read, yet we spread them out over days and weeks. How much of your novel's plot would you grasp if you only read it five minutes a day? I encourage you to try reading the Bible a whole book at a time. You don't need to start at Genesis and go straight through. (Most people who try that don't get past the middle of Leviticus!) Pick whatever looks interesting, but read it like an article or any other book. Read until you get to something that makes you stop and think or pray. Then stop and think and pray! If you can, write down what you thought or prayed about. God made it stand out to you for a reason, so you don't want to forget it.

One of the best things about the Bible is that any time we want, the divine author makes himself available to us, to answer our questions and guide our understanding. That means the first and most important step in Bible reading is to pray and listen.

Pray for God to guide you in what to read. Pray for him to help you understand the meaning of what you read. Pray for him to show you how it applies to your life. Pray for God to tell you what he wants you to do about it. And pray for him to grant you faith and wisdom in stepping out to do it. Then, as you read, don't forget to listen for answers to your prayer. Ask God to help you be open to receive the ideas he may whisper to your spirit.

Sometimes it's more than a whisper. I have read through the Bible a number of times. Some passages I have probably read thousands of times. Yet it is amazing how often I'll suddenly see a new meaning or application in something I've read many times before. Sometimes it's almost as if the words jump off the page, grab me by the scruff of the neck, and say, "Hey, I'm talking to you!"

We should approach the Bible differently than other books, because it alone is the inspired word of God to his people. But the difference should be in our attitude of reverence and trust, not in how we understand the meaning. When you read a book, there are some basic rules that help us grasp what the author is saying. Most of the time these are so ingrained into us that we don't even notice we're doing it. Occasionally, when we hit something we don't immediately understand, we consciously employ these rules. God put his message to us in a book, so when we hit a hard part, we should employ the same rules. Here's a quick summary.

Context

There is a saying in real estate that the three most important things are location, location, and location. In understanding written texts, the key is context, context, and context.

What is the literary context? Do the surrounding sentences or story line shed any light on the meaning? Let the Bible interpret the Bible.

What is the historical context? Things were going on in the world at the time which the original readers would have been well aware of but we might not. Does that help us understand?

What is the cultural context? Were there traditions or customs that might explain what is being said?

Genre

Different types or genres of writing are meant to be understood in different ways. What kind of writing is the passage you are looking at? The Bible contains several kinds of writing we encounter all the time, such as history, poetry, legal writing, stories, and letters. It also contains prophetic and apocalyptic writing, which are not so common today. If you try to interpret a piece of poetry as if it were a legal brief, you are likely to miss the meaning.

Figures of speech

In John 10:9, Jesus said, *I am the gate*. In John 15:5 he said, *I am the vine*. Was Jesus a shape-shifter, changing form from a gate to a vine? Is this one of those contradictions some people claim the Bible is full of? Or was he just crazy? I'm being facetious, of course, because we all understand Jesus was not literally claiming to be a gate or a vine; he was using a figure of speech. Sometimes that is also the explanation for other passages that are not so obvious.

Most of the time, recognizing figures of speech, genre, and context will go a long way toward helping you understand what God is saying. A good study Bible or commentary, in print or online, can be very helpful with all these.

How to Prepare A Message

What we just said about reading and understanding the Bible applies to every Christian, all the time. Preparing a sermon or message for others to hear is a much more specific and responsible task. Here are five steps to guide you through it.

Pray and listen

As always, the first step is to pray, and listen for God's answer. What does God want to say? What is God's message for your listeners? How does God want you to convey that message so your listeners can best hear, understand, receive, and act on what God is saying?

Notice I said, "What God is saying," not, "What you want to tell them." This is not about your own ideas or opinions. There is a place for those, and sometimes you can bring them into a sermon if you clearly label them as your own thoughts. But your main task here is to let God speak through you. Have faith that if you are truly seeking God, he will use you — yes, even you! — to say what he wants your listeners to hear. So ask God to guide you, trust that he will, and do your best.

Once you have an idea of God's message for your hearers, prayerfully ask God to show you how you can best present it. Is there a certain passage of the Bible that pretty much says what God wants you to get across? If so, an expository sermon might be best, where you explain the passage verse by verse. Does God want you to tell people what he has said about a certain topic? Find places in the Bible that address those and pull them together into a topical sermon. Perhaps the message is one that can best be illustrated by a story from the Bible or history or your own experience, or even one you make up. That is called a narrative sermon.

The type of sermon depends not only on what fits the message, but on your own personality as well. I know Jesus told a lot of stories when he preached, and I know many people learn best through stories. But that is just not the way I think. I can tell a good story when I need to, but I have to work at it. The point is, no sermon type or preaching style is better than another. The best is whatever fits your message, your personality, and your hearers.

Research

Unless you plan to just talk off the top of your head — something even the most experienced pastors try to avoid — you will need to do some research. You probably won't use everything you find, but it's a lot easier to not say something you have learned than to say something you haven't.

Most people's idea of research is to look up what somebody else has written. That's a natural impulse, and perhaps in everything other than Bible study it makes sense. But with the Bible, you have the author right there to ask. The Holy Spirit, who inspired the writers of the Scriptures, is living inside every Christian to inspire their understanding of his words. Not only that, but the Holy Spirit inspired the different writers of the Bible, in different ages and different cultures, to address many of the same topics. So your first step is to let the Bible explain the Bible. Here's how.

Most Bibles contain cross-references to other passages that talk about the same thing. When you run across something hard to understand, your first step is to follow the cross-references to see if they make it clearer. Some people call that "running the references." They are usually indicated by a little superscript letter or number in the text of your Bible verse. Look for the same letter or number in the margin, and it will list related verses. If you are not using a print Bible, looking up cross references is even easier. Most Bible study programs and websites will take you right to a cross reference with a simple click. Just be sure at this stage of your study that you are mainly looking at what the other verses in the Bible have to say, rather than someone else's commentary. Remember, the Bible is inspired; the commentary and footnotes are not.

As you compare verses, sometimes it may seem hard to see how some of them fit together. If this happens, remember, God does not contradict himself. If it seems like something in the Bible contradicts something else in the Bible, or contradicts a fact of science or history, there are three possibilities.

1. You may not correctly understand what the Bible is saying, in one or both places.
2. You may not correctly understand what science or history are saying.
3. The current scientific or historical understanding may be wrong (we all know how often theories change and new discoveries are announced).

It may be that running the references is all you need in the way of research. Still, it never hurts at this point to read what other educated, prayerful Christians have written throughout the ages. You will find these thoughts in study Bibles, commentaries, and Bible dictionaries or encyclopedias. Commentaries are books that seek to explain the Bible verse by verse and passage by passage. Bible dictionaries and Bible encyclopedias contain articles about topics, places, and people. If you want to go deeper, there are special books and resources that help you dig into the original languages of the Bible, even if you don't know a letter of Hebrew, Aramaic, or Greek. Study Bibles include information from all these along with the Bible text.

The internet makes all of this extremely easy. There are some excellent free Bible study tools readily available online, and you should take advantage of them. Of course, you can't accept everything you find on the internet. I address that a little more in Appendix 2.

Think

You found your topic or passage, you've done your research, now you are ready to start writing a sermon, right? Not so fast! There's a very important step you have to do first (one I too often skip in many areas of life): think!

As the saying goes, "God gave you your head for more than a hat rack."

God told Moses to build him a tabernacle and showed him the general plan, but he left the details to the creativity of Bezalel and his coworkers. God told Noah to build him a ship. He specified the dimensions and materials, but he left Noah to figure out how to go about it. God gives us direction through our spirits, but for the details, he expects us to use our brains. So don't rush this step.

> *Study this Book of Instruction continually. Meditate on it day and night so you will be sure to obey everything written in it. Only then will you prosper and succeed in all you do.* (Joshua 1:8)

The "Book of Instruction," of course, is the Bible. Joshua only had the first part; we are blessed with the whole thing. So what does it mean to meditate on the Bible?

Meditation, in the Biblical sense, doesn't mean chanting "Om, Om" while you gaze at your navel. Meditation means prayerful contemplation. It means to think deeply, chew something over in your mind. In fact, the term originally comes from same word that describes a cow chewing its cud.

Like some parts of the Bible, grass is tough stuff to digest. To deal with it, God gave cows four stomachs. When a cow first eats grass she swallows it down into her first stomach, which is a kind of holding tank until she is done grazing. Later on, while she's resting, she brings the grass back up from that first stomach, a little bit at a time, and chews it more thoroughly. This is called "chewing its cud." Then she swallows it down into her second stomach, and it goes on through the digestive process. Cows and other animals that chew cud are called "ruminants," because the technical word for chewing cud is "ruminating."

Interestingly, in the English language, "ruminate" is also a synonym for "meditate." When you first read a Bible passage or come across an idea or concept, you may get something out of it. But if you leave it at that point, you are likely to miss a lot. Instead, "swallow it into the first stomach" of your memory. Then, when you have a chance — taking a walk, or driving, or as you are falling asleep or waking up — recall it to your mind, like a cow bringing the grass back out of her first stomach, and chew it over, think about it some more. We should always have some scripture passages in reserve for meditation. As God told Joshua, that is a major key to success in life.

When you are preparing a message, it is important to meditate on the scriptures you will be using. But there are some other things you should think about as well.

1. How well do you yourself understand the message God wants you too convey? Make sure you have it clear in your own mind before you try to help others get it into theirs.
2. How familiar are your hearers with the topic? How much will you have to explain?
3. How can you best illustrate your points?
4. What do you believe God wants the people to do with this information? How can you motivate them or give them an opportunity to do it?
5. What questions might people have, and how can you answer them in your presentation?

When you have thought all that through, you are almost done.

Arrange

The next to last step is to put everything into some kind of order that makes sense.

If you are presenting facts and drawing a conclusion, you want people to be able to follow your reasoning. If you are telling a story, don't give away the ending, unless your overall message works better that way.

Answer the questions that will arise in people's minds as they listen. Sometimes it's easiest and clearest just to walk people through your own process of discovery and reasoning. Tell them what got you thinking about this, the questions you had, how you found the answers, and what you believe God is telling you about it all.

Add stories or illustrations where they will help make things clear. Don't add them when they don't. It is tempting to use a story or joke just because it is moving or funny. If it doesn't add to your message, file it away to use another time. You don't want to get people thinking about other things and losing sight of your main point.

Give concrete examples of how what you are saying applies to everyday life. Your mission is not just to impart knowledge, it's to help people grow more like Jesus.

Don't try to say too much. One or two points is all you need. If you have more than three you will lose people.

End with a call to action. What do you want people to do with what you have told them? If it is something internal or personal, like a period of self-reflection, prayer, or study, consider suggesting some kind of accountability. If your group includes prayer partners, you can encourage them to ask each other about it, or you can make follow-up part of what you do at the next gathering. If it is something that is better done as a group, like a community service project, you might move into a discussion of how, when, and where. It is not enough to just leave people saying, "Well, that was interesting." Give them something to do about it.

As with paraphrasing someone else's message, you may want to write out a full manuscript, or you may feel comfortable talking from notes or an outline. There is no right or wrong way to do it. Whatever works best for you is fine.

Pray some more

The last step is the same as the first: pray. Pray about your own understanding of the message God wants you to give. Pray about the way you will express it. Pray for people's understanding, and a godly response. Keep up the prayers, right up until you begin speaking. And in response to your prayers, be open to revising what you are saying and how you are saying it, even as you are talking.

APPENDIX 1: SERMONS IN A NUTSHELL

How to Give a Message

Meeting with a small group in the living room gives you much more freedom in how to present your message than a preacher in the pulpit of a conventional church may have. You can use a traditional lecture-type sermon format if you choose, but you are not limited to that. There are at least two other good options you should consider.

In a guided study, you prepare the message pretty much as we have been talking about, but you don't present it as a lecture. Instead, you prepare questions to ask your listeners as you go along, so your listeners bring out the points you want to make. Instead of reading a Bible passage and just talking about it, you might ask someone else to read the passage. Then your questions can lead people through the same thought process you followed in your preparations, to the conclusions you already reached in your study. In other words, instead of giving your hearers a list of points, you guide the discussion to bring out the points from the hearers.

In a discussion format, everyone participates in an open conversation about the topic or passage. As leader, you prepare, but you keep most of the information in reserve in case questions come up. In this case, you guide the discussion as little as possible. Instead, you have three tasks. First, keep the conversation on topic. Second, keep the conversation balanced — encourage quiet people to share their thoughts, and talkative people to give others a chance. And, of course, keep an eye on the time. If by the end something you wanted to get across has not come up, you can decide whether just to tell everybody, or let it go until another time.

Let me insert a quick word of warning here about the last two formats. Be careful about asking, "What does this mean to you?" Especially in America, land of equality, we like to think that everyone's ideas are equally valid. In some things they may be, but not in understanding the Bible. In Bible study the question is not, "What does this mean to you?" but "What does this mean to God?" That's one reason you have done your research. Throughout history, well-intentioned people have come up with all kinds of crazy ideas about certain passages of the Bible. We will look at that more in Appendix

2. If you choose to present your message through guided discussion or free conversation, one of your jobs is to know the historically accepted Christian understanding(s) of a passage or topic (there may be more than one), and be prepared to explain why other ideas are wrong.

However you choose to bring your message, at least until you have done it for a while, practice. When I first started, we practiced in front of a mirror. Nowadays, it is easy to set up your phone or tablet and record video of yourself. I encourage you to do this, and then go back and carefully watch it. When I first did that, after years of preaching, I was amazed at how distracting some of my gestures could be. Make sure all your movements, facial expressions, and other mannerisms help people focus on and understand what you are saying. Listen for how your voice sounds. In particular, do you drop your voice in volume at the end of a sentence or a paragraph? Most of us do this more often than we realize, often to the point where people may not even be able to hear the last words.

Appendix 2: Potential Problems

We know that God causes everything to work together for the good of those who love God and are called according to His purpose for them. — Romans 8:28

I know what you may be thinking. "I knew this home church stuff couldn't all be as easy and upbeat as the rest of this book makes it sound. You hide all the problems back here in the Appendix, hoping we won't see them!"

The fact is, every human endeavor is going to have problems. Working with God and God's people is no different. This Appendix lists some problems that may arise in Christian home gatherings, in hopes that "forewarned is forearmed."

Differences in Practice

As long as your motives are right, there is basically no wrong way to gather as followers of Jesus. If you are seeking to honor and worship God, and you aren't doing anything the Bible specifically says not to, like worshiping idols or having seances, it is pretty much impossible to go wrong. There are some things that are pretty much essential for any kind of Christian church or worship gathering. We've already looked at those. But the Bible gives remarkably little guidance as to exactly how we are supposed to put all these things together.

"But what if we do it differently from some other group? What if our meetings don't go the same way as theirs?"

If you notice, the other groups you are looking at do things differently from each other as well. It's not like everyone is doing it the right way and if you do it differently, you are wrong. Most of it is a matter of preference, or differences of opinion about how to apply certain Bible verses.

You can certainly see this with conventional churches. Some worship with an organ and choir, others use a praise band. Some read written prayers, others pray spontaneously. Some stand when they pray, some pray sitting down, and some kneel. Each church can point to Bible verses they believe support their practice, but very rarely does the Bible explicitly say we are supposed to do it one way and not another. Different groups of good, Bible-believing Christians have different ways of doing things. I believe God is fine with that.

Differences in Belief

Different groups of good, Bible believing Christians not only do things differently, they also see certain issues differently. I believe God is fine with that, too. Most of these differences are matters of biblical interpretation, where some verses seem to support one view, and others support a slightly different perspective. These are not contradictions within the Bible; these are insufficiencies in our understanding. One day in heaven we will see the whole picture, and we will see how our different views all fit together into God's glorious truth.

Here are a few of the common areas where good Christians differ:

- Predestination versus free will
- "Once saved, always saved" versus the possibility of losing salvation
- Infant baptism versus believer's baptism
- Whether certain activities, such as drinking or going to movies, are acceptable for Christians
- Exactly what is going to happen in the end times

John Wesley, founder of the Methodist movement, said, "In all things that do not strike at the heart of Christian faith, we think and let think." It's not a new idea. St. Augustine, 1300 years earlier, put it this way: "In essentials, unity; in non-essentials, liberty; in all things, love."

Those two quotes give us a lot of freedom. But they also imply that there are some things that are essential, things that are at the heart of Christian faith. Those things we do have to get right. Because if you make serious mistakes about eternal truths, then you are messing with people's souls and their eternal destiny.

Honest Mistakes

The apostle Paul wrote to his protege, Timothy, *Now the Holy Spirit tells us clearly that in the last times some will turn away from the true faith; they will follow deceptive spirits and teachings that come from demons* (1 Timothy 4:1).

It's one thing to rebel against God and go your own way. People who do that know what they are doing, and it's their choice. It is something else entirely to be deceived, to be led away from the truth and buy into ideas that seem reasonable and even Biblical but are not. This can happen even when we are trying our best. As the old saying reminds us, good intentions don't always pave the road to good places.

Unfortunately, it can be easy to make an honest mistake about God questions, because the Bible is not always as clear as we would like. On the essentials it is; that's one way of knowing what God considers really important. But in many areas it is easy to come up with ideas that sound logical, but which Christian theologians of all stripes have understood throughout history as not being quite right. The technical term for a dangerously wrong theological idea is "heresy." The ability to detect incipient heresy before it becomes a problem is one of the main reasons it is important for your group to have some kind of relationship with a trained pastor, who knows something about theology and church history.

Here is a quick run-down of some of the more common mistakes.

The Nature of God

The relationship between God and Jesus and the Holy Spirit is hard to understand, especially in light of the clear Biblical teaching that there is only one God. So some have reasoned this way: "The Bible calls Jesus the Son of God. A son is separate from his father, and at least for the first part of his life he's smaller and weaker. So 'Son of God' must mean Jesus is a separate, lesser god, and not eternal. The Holy Spirit must be a lesser god, too — or maybe just an impersonal force." That sounds logical, but it is actually an ancient heresy called Arianism, that violates the historical Christian teaching of the Trinity. The Jehovah's Witnesses follow a form of that today.

Another way of trying to deal with the same question is to conclude that sometimes God is the Father, and other times he is Jesus, and other times he is the Holy Spirit. Again, it sounds logical, but for a variety of Biblical and theological reasons it is not considered orthodox Christian doctrine. God is Trinity, three persons in one God, always and forever.

Some feel the Bible depicts God in the Old Testament as wrathful and judgmental, and in the New Testament as loving and merciful. As far back as the second century, a teacher named Marcion tried to explain that by saying they were two different gods. A more modern explanation is to say that there is only the one God, but the Old Testament writers were wrong in how they described him. Again, neither of these ideas is in line with historically accepted Christian teaching, which says different parts of the Bible emphasize different aspects of the one and only true God.

The Nature of Jesus

Some parts of the Bible describe Jesus as human. Others describe him as divine. In trying to reconcile the two, it might seem logical to think that perhaps Jesus just pretended to be human, as if his human body was just a kind of costume or disguise. That also seems to answer another logical conundrum that asks, "If Jesus is God and he really died on the cross, then didn't God die? And if God died, who was running the universe, and who raised him from the dead?" Some feel that if Jesus was just pretending to be human, and it was just a costume that died on the cross, those problems go away. The trouble is, salvation goes away as well, because the whole point of Jesus dying on the cross and rising again is that he did it as one of us. The idea that Jesus just seemed or pretended to be human is actually an ancient heresy called docetism.

Praise the Lord, God is not subject to the limitations of human logical constructs. Jesus is fully human and fully divine. As to exactly how that works, as my military friends say, "That's above my pay grade."

The Nature of Humans

Ancient Greek philosophers taught that human beings are invisible spirits trapped in physical bodies. They said if we gain certain spiritual knowledge, and we believe it hard enough, then the superior reality of the mind/spirit realm will overcome whatever is happening in our bodies and the world. That idea infiltrated into early Christianity in a heresy called Gnosticism. You can see a modern form of the same thing in Christian Science and in extreme forms of what is often called "the power of positive thinking."

Some carry it further and conclude, "Once your spirit is born again, that's what counts. Your body is just temporary physical stuff; what happens to it really isn't important. So go have fun! Do whatever you want to with your body." That is clearly not Biblical Christian teaching.

Jesus showed the eternal importance to God of the physical side of our humanity when he took it on himself as a baby. Not only that, he was raised from the dead in a physical body (Luke 24:35-42). God created human beings in God's own image. *In the image of God he created them; male and female he created them* (Genesis 1:27). Part of that image was creating us as a human trinity of body, soul, and spirit, in one person. (Your soul includes your mind and emotions.) God expects us to honor him in all parts of our being. Jesus said, *You must love the Lord your God with all your heart, all your soul, all your mind, and all your strength* (Mark 12:30).

How We Know Things

God loves us, God knows everything, and God always wants what is best for us. He wanted to communicate that to us in a way that would provide a lasting, objective standard available to everyone. The best format for that kind of communication down through the ages has proven to be a book. God gave us such a book, and we call it the Bible. Our primary source for spiritual truth and revelation about God is the Bible.

If we ask, God also gives us specific guidance for our individual situations, through answered prayer and through the exercise of some of the spiritual gifts (see 1 Corinthians 12). Science and other academic disciplines are good gifts from God that also help us discover new knowledge. Unfortunately, sometimes we are so impressed with new revelations or discoveries that we let them supersede what the Bible says. This is a huge mistake.

We see this mistake in two main forms today. One sounds like this: "I know that down through the last 2000 years every major Christian group has believed these verses mean this, but God showed me a new revelation that they actually mean this other thing." The idea that some contemporary, subjective spiritual experience is as authoritative as the Bible is an old heresy called Montanism.

The other form of this mistake is the belief that new scientific or theological ideas trump the Bible. Science and theology should certainly inform our understanding, but they are always evolving. Where there seem to be contradictions, we need to deal with them as I outlined in Appendix 1.

What It Takes to Get to Heaven

One of the major areas where well-intentioned people can get off track has to do with what it takes to get to heaven.

A misunderstanding of the relationship between the Old and New Testaments can lead to the idea that in order to be acceptable to God you have to follow the whole Mosaic Law. In other words, males have to be circumcised, you can't eat pork, and so on. There are strong arguments against this in the Bible itself, particularly in the book of Acts and in Paul's letters, but it has remained remarkably persistent. In later centuries it was known as the Ebionite heresy.

The Ebionite heresy is one version of the idea that the ticket to heaven is good deeds. It is true that the Bible in many places describes the kind of life a good Christian should live. However, it is also clear that this new life is a result of being born again, not the means to it. The idea that human beings can or must earn their way into heaven by their own efforts, apart from God's grace, is a heresy called Pelagianism.

The other side of that is an overemphasis on the verses that say Christ fulfilled the law for us, such as Galatians 3:10-13. Some people stretch that truth to say there are no longer any boundaries or standards and we can do whatever we feel like. That heresy is called antinomianism.

Combine a sentimental view of God's love with a misunderstanding of the rest of God's character and you get the appealing idea that everybody will wind up in heaven eventually no matter what they believe or how they have lived, because God is just too nice to send anyone to hell. This heresy is called universalism.

The laudable modern emphasis on tolerance and inclusivity has led many to the idea that all religions lead to God. In that view, true religion is "whatever works for you." This makes religious faith totally subjective — which means it has no objective reality. It also leads to the idea that you can mix Christian ideas with ideas from other religions: "Let's call ourselves Christian, but let's include a little bit of reincarnation, or karma, or spiritualism." This is called syncretism.

The Bible is clear.

> *God saved you by his grace when you believed. And you can't take credit for this; it is a gift from God. Salvation is not a reward for the good things we have done, so none of us can boast about it (Ephesians 2:8–9).*
>
> *Just as the body is dead without breath, so also faith is dead without good works (James 2:26).*

The End Times

Different ideas about the end times are not heretical, but they can lead to problems.

One of the first Christian books I read, way back in the early 1970s, was called *The Late Great Planet Earth*, by Hal Lindsey. It laid out in specific detail exactly what will happen when Jesus returns, all backed up with Scripture. When I finished that book everything was so clear! I understood biblical prophecy perfectly. I knew exactly what was going to happen.

Then I made a mistake: I read another book about the end times. It made just as clear and biblical a case that things will happen in an entirely different way. I've been confused about the end times ever since!

About that same time, some people started a Bible study group in a church I knew. I am all in favor of Bible study groups, but this one started focusing on one particular view of end times prophecy. They became convinced that Jesus was just about to come back. The pastor could have given some perspective and possible correction, but they didn't ask him. Before he knew what was happening, several of the families had quit their jobs, sold their homes, and moved together to a mountain in Georgia to wait for Jesus to come back.

I don't know what happened to them. But I do know two things. First, I would have checked things out with someone outside the group before I quit my job and sold my house. And second, that was almost 50 years ago, and Jesus still hasn't come back.

Some things in the Bible are clear, but how the end times will unfold is not one of them. I believe God intended it that way.

Guideposts

For most of what you do as a group, if you do it differently from some other group, that's fine. But as we saw above, there are certain ideas about the Bible and doctrine that seem reasonable, but can really get you off track. So how do you know if a teaching or Bible interpretation is going in a dangerous direction?

There is a wonderful promise in Isaiah 30:21: *Your own ears will hear him. Right behind you a voice will say, "This is the way you should go," whether to the right or to the left.* God doesn't want his children going in a wrong direction and getting lost. If we start to do that, he warns us in our spirits. If something doesn't feel right to you, pay attention to that feeling. It might be God giving you a warning.

Of course, you can't just say, "This makes me uncomfortable. I'm outta here!" Sometimes God's truths do feel uncomfortable, especially to our old human nature. If someone in your group brings a message you don't like, don't take that as a sign that you should confront them, or denounce them, or leave the group. But don't just shrug it off, either. Take it as a sign that maybe God wants you to check it out further. After all, more delving into the Bible and Christian belief is always a good thing, right?

Here are three guideposts that can help keep us safe.

The Bible

First, compare the new idea to the rest of the Bible. As we said in a previous chapter, since the whole Bible is inspired by God, and God does not contradict himself, then the Bible, properly understood, will not contradict itself.

Verifying a teaching in this way does not indicate skepticism or lack of faith. In fact, the Bible says it's a sign of nobility! *Now the Berean Jews were of more noble character than those in Thessalonica, for they received the message with great eagerness and examined the Scriptures every day to see if what Paul said was true* (Acts 17:11, NIV).

The Apostles Creed

If comparing Bible verses doesn't make things clear, compare the new idea to what faithful Christians down through the ages have believed. A simple way to do that is to see whether it conflicts with any point of the Apostles Creed.

A creed is a brief summary of the essential beliefs of a religion or other group. For Christians, the best known of these is the Apostles Creed, so called because it summarizes the basic elements of what the apostles taught. It is officially recognized by many different denominations and groups as a way of defining the basic essential beliefs of the Christian faith. If you grew up in a mainline liturgical church, you probably know it, because many of those churches recite it regularly in their services — and that is not a bad idea.

The Apostles Creed doesn't include everything that every Christian denomination believes. But if a teaching or idea conflicts with any part of the Apostles Creed, that means it is not compatible with historical standards of true Christianity.

Here is the most commonly used version of the Apostles Creed. Other versions vary slightly in wording (such as "sitteth" instead of "is seated"), but no point of meaning is affected.

> I believe in God, the Father Almighty,
>   creator of heaven and earth.
> I believe in Jesus Christ, his only Son, our Lord,
>   who was conceived by the Holy Spirit,
>   born of the Virgin Mary,
>   suffered under Pontius Pilate,
>   was crucified, died, and was buried;
>   he descended to the dead.
>   On the third day he rose again;
>   he ascended into heaven,
>   is seated at the right hand of the Father,
>   and will come again to judge the living and the dead.
> I believe in the Holy Spirit,
>   the holy catholic ["universal"] church,
>   the communion of saints,
>   the forgiveness of sins,
>   the resurrection of the body,
>   and the life everlasting. Amen.

If a Biblical interpretation or theological idea contradicts one of those points, take it very skeptically. Try to have these basic principals so thoroughly soaked into your mind and heart that if something is wrong, you will immediately know it.

Research

What if something doesn't sound quite right, but you can't place your finger on how it conflicts with the Bible or an accepted point of Christian teaching? Don't just let it go. Dig a little deeper.

Up until recently, digging deeper meant hours in the theological section of a good library. Nowadays, all you have to do is type your question into an internet search engine. That is a wonderful gift of God. But use it wisely. False teachings and mistakes can have their own websites.

How do you know which websites you can trust? Most reliable Christian websites:

1. Quote the Bible (a lot!)
2. Post a statement of belief that aligns with the Apostles Creed and the statements of belief of other good ministry websites
3. Don't charge money, at least for their basic services

Be wary of websites that:

1. Claim some new revelation that nobody else has
2. Attack other Christian ministries, groups, or denominations
3. Promise spiritual benefits if you send them money

Wolves in Sheep's Clothing

Anyone can make an honest mistake. Wolves in sheep's clothing are entirely different. I'm talking about people who try to get into a group and take it over. Sometimes that is just a power trip. But sometimes they deliberately try to lead you into false teaching. Often they believe it themselves. But just because they are sincere doesn't mean they are right. They can be just as deceived as they are trying to make you.

When Paul passed through Ephesus the last time, the Lord had already told him he was going to be arrested. He knew he may never see the Ephesian Christians again. So he gathered together the leaders of the home fellowships there. One of the things he told them was,

> *I know that false teachers, like vicious wolves, will come in among you after I leave, not sparing the flock. Even some men from your own group will rise up and distort the truth in order to draw a following. Watch out!* (Acts 20:29–31)

How can you recognize when that is happening?

Recognizing wolves

First, look at what the new person is trying to get you to believe. If it is something like we just talked about, it could just be an honest mistake. In that case, a godly person will humbly accept correction, and be grateful that you warned them. If they get angry or arrogantly insist on their authority, that's a big red flag.

Second, look at the person's life. Do they demonstrate the character of Jesus and lead you to God? Or do they seek money or glory for themselves? Are there any warning signs in their past that you can find out about? Jesus said, *Just as you can identify a tree by its fruit, so you can identify people by their actions* (Matthew 7:20). You will know them by what shows in their lives and their past history.

Paul tells us specifically what to look for.

> *When you follow the desires of your sinful nature, the results are very clear: sexual immorality, impurity, lustful pleasures, idolatry, sorcery, hostility, quarreling, jealousy, outbursts of anger, selfish ambition,*

dissension, division, envy, drunkenness, wild parties, and other sins like these. Let me tell you again, as I have before, that anyone living that sort of life will not inherit the Kingdom of God. But the Holy Spirit produces this kind of fruit in our lives: love, joy, peace, patience, kindness, goodness, faithfulness, gentleness, and self-control. There is no law against these things! (Galatians 5:19–23)

Dealing with wolves

What do you do if you realize that one of these wolves in sheep's clothing has infiltrated your group? We have instructions from Jesus himself.

If another believer sins against you, go privately and point out the offense. If the other person listens and confesses it, you have won that person back. But if you are unsuccessful, take one or two others with you and go back again, so that everything you say may be confirmed by two or three witnesses. If the person still refuses to listen, take your case to the church. Then if he or she won't accept the church's decision, treat that person as a pagan or a corrupt tax collector. (Matthew 18:15–17)

This process is not restricted to protecting your home group. It applies every time a Christian feels wrongly treated by another believer. That can happen a lot! So let's look at it a little more closely.

If another believer sins against you. Coming into your group and trying to lead you away from the truth clearly qualifies as a sin against you.

Go privately and point out the offense. If the other person listens and confesses it, you have won that person back. Start privately. It could be they are honestly mistaken, and they will be glad to be corrected.

But if you are unsuccessful, take one or two others with you and go back again, so that everything you say may be confirmed by two or three witnesses. What if you privately confront them and they don't listen to you, but you still prayerfully believe you are right and they are wrong? Prayerfully discuss the situation with one or two mature Christians you respect. At least one should be a member of your group. Another might be an experienced pastor or church leader who can give you a wider perspective. If they don't see the issue the same way you do, maybe you are wrong and you should drop it. But if they agree with you, take them back with you, or at least the one who is part of your group, and talk to the person again.

If the person still refuses to listen, take your case to the church. Now there are two or three of you who believe this person is wrong, but the person still won't admit it. If you still prayerfully feel God is leading you to pursue the issue, it's time to bring the matter before the rest of your group. Prayerfully and carefully present the concerns. If the group agrees there is a problem, but the person still says, "Nope, you're all wrong," you move on to the final step.

Then if he or she won't accept the church's decision, treat that person as a pagan or a corrupt tax collector. In other words, treat them the same way you would treat any person who would scoff at your beliefs and try to lead you away from your faith.

John tells us,

> *If anyone comes to your meeting and does not teach the truth about Christ, don't invite that person into your home or give any kind of encouragement. Anyone who encourages such people becomes a partner in their evil work* (2 John 10–11).

And Paul, referring to a specific instance that was actually happening at the time in the church in Corinth, wrote, *You should remove this man from your fellowship* (Corinthians 5:2).

You may be thinking, "Wow! That seems pretty drastic! What about tolerance and open doors and everybody's welcome and all of that?" Those are great values for an evangelistic crusade, but that is not what we are talking about here. We are talking about a small fellowship of people gathered in our house to worship the Lord and grow more like Jesus. In that setting, if somebody is trying to take us in a different direction and doesn't allow themselves to be corrected, they can easily destroy the group, and possibly our faith. That is why Jesus and John and Paul all recommend protective action.

Calling in back-up

I have said you don't need someone with a seminary degree to lead your group, and that is true. But it is good to have a relationship with somebody who has training in theology and church history, and experience in leading Christians. They can look at some of these things and say, "You know, back in the sixth century, this group started saying such and so and it sounded okay at the beginning, but it led to these problems." They might see little issues that are not a problem now, but that could develop into trouble if they are not corrected.

God's Got Your Back

I don't want to scare you. The kinds of issues we have been discussing are very rare. The vast majority of home groups never have to deal with anything like this.

There is really no wrong way for a small group of Christians to gather together to seek the Lord. About the only thing that can go wrong is to start following an idea that could lead to a problem. Now you know what to look for, so you can stop it.

No matter what happens, we have this wonderful promise: *We know that God causes everything to work together for the good of those who love God and are called according to his purpose for them* (Romans 8:28). I call that my safety-net verse. You are meeting together to worship God and grow like Jesus. Obviously, you love God and are called according to his purpose. That means you can count on this promise. God will cause everything to work together for your good. God is not going to let you go off in a wrong direction, if you are seeking to honor him and follow his guidance.

About the Author

Thirty-eight years as a pastor honed David's passion for helping people connect with God and make a difference. Add a varied church background, a first career in engineering, and graduate degrees from three seminaries (mainstream, Wesleyan-evangelical, and charismatic), and you can see why he expresses God's truth in ways everyone can appreciate.

Raised in the Episcopal church, David has also been part of Nazarene, Pentecostal Holiness, and non-denominational congregations. As a United Methodist pastor he has served small, large, and multi-cultural churches in rural, small town, suburban and urban settings. He served as a regional church consultant in the Maryland – D.C. area, and led workshops for pastors in Turkey. In 2019 David founded Doing Christianity, Inc., a non-profit organization dedicated to equipping pastors in developing and minority-Christian countries.

David married his college sweetheart, Paula, in 1974. Their five children are actively serving God in the US and around the world.

David earned a B.S. in Systems Engineering from the University of Virginia; two Masters of Divinity, from Melodyland School of Theology and Wesley Theological Seminary, and a Doctor of Ministry from Asbury Theological Seminary. He enjoys the outdoors, reading, and playing music. His heroes are John Wesley, Abraham Lincoln, and Martin Luther King, Jr.

An outline of Ezekiel describes David's calling: to equip God's people by teaching God's words and proclaiming the Holy Spirit, who revives dry bones and forms them into a dwelling for God and a source of the living water that heals nations.

Bones are still dry, the Holy Spirit is still active, God still desires to dwell with his people, and nations still need healing.

You can connect with me on:
- https://www.pastordavidwentz.com
- https://www.facebook.com/Pastor-David-Wentz

Subscribe to my newsletter:
- https://mailchi.mp/c162e27f817b/doing-christianity-email-newsletter-sign-up

Also by David Wentz

Pastoring: The Nuts and Bolts
Options and Best Practices for Being a Pastor and Leading a Church

Pastoring: The Nuts and Bolts began when pastors in Turkey asked for a written version of Dr. Wentz's workshops. Now it has been translated into five languages, and thousands of copies have been donated to train pastors in Africa and Asia.

Designed especially for pastors looking for help with day to day ministry issues, it stands out from similar books in its comprehensive scope and theological and cultural neutrality, including issues common to charismatic and pentecostal as well as mainline and evangelical churches around the world. It offers options and best practices rather than prescriptions. If a pastor or church can have only one book besides the Bible, this is designed to be most helpful.

Pastoring: The Nuts and Bolts — Application Guide
Create a customized action plan for your church!

Full of thoughtful questions and exercises, this *Application Guide* takes the general principles from *Pastoring: The Nuts and Bolts,* and makes them yours. Some questions will make you think and pray about what you believe and why. Others will take you from, "Hey, that's a good idea!" to "Here's an action plan for my church.

Every time your ministry changes, these exercises will give you a brand new strategy, customized by you for your specific situation, ready to implement.

John Wesley's The Character of a Methodist
Set in Modern Language with Introduction and Suggestions for Group Use

In a time of upheaval in the largest denomination of the Methodist movement, this classic explanation and defense of Methodist Christianity by its founder is required reading. Pastor David Wentz has updated Wesley's 18th-century language, deleted references to no-longer-relevant theological disputes, and added an introduction that sets the work in context. The result is a clear, easy to read text that is enjoyable and understandable for modern readers of all levels of theological interest and expertise.

This short book is ideal for small groups and adult Sunday School classes as well as individual reading. Dr. Wentz has included thoughtful discussion questions at the end of each section, a brief guide on how to lead small groups, and a suggested six-week schedule. For further study, Wesley's numerous Scripture quotes and allusions are identified, with the Biblical text cited and quoted in footnotes. Wesley's full original version is included as an appendix.

No matter where one stands in the wide umbrella of worldwide Methodism, this accessible summary of its root emphases provides a vital foundation.

www.ingramcontent.com/pod-product-compliance
Lightning Source LLC
Chambersburg PA
CBHW060359080526
44583CB00012B/380